D1272480

atlas of
FASHION designers

LAURA ECEIZA

ROCKPORT

atlas of
FASHION designers

LAURA ECEIZA

BEVERLY MASSACHUSETTS

ROCKPORT PUBLISHERS

Copyright © 2008 by **maomao** publications
First published in 2008 in the United States of America by
Rockport Publishers, a member of
Quayside Publishing Group
100 Cummings Center
Suite 406-L
Beverly, MA 01915-6101
Telephone: (978) 282-9590
Fax: (978) 283-2742
www.rockpub.com

ISBN-13: 978-1-59253-429-6
ISBN-10: 1-59253-429-5

Publisher: Paco Asensio

Editorial coordination: Anja Llorella Oriol

Editor: Laura Eceiza Nebreda

Text: Laura Eceiza Nebreda, María Asensio Álvarez

Editorial assistant: Rayén Torres Pabón, Hugo Gallego Illana

Art director: Emma Termes Parera

Graphic design and layout: Maira Purman, Zahira Rodríguez Mediavila

English translation: Kevin Krell

Editorial project:
maomao publications
Tallers, 22 bis, 3º 1ª
08001 Barcelona, Spain
Tel.: +34 93 481 57 22
Fax: +34 93 317 42 08
www.maomaopublications.com

Printed in China

Fashion Identity, Diversity and Design Around the World

Photography by Ian Guillet

Fashion Identity, Diversity and Design Around the World

The traditional demarcation line of fashion—London, Paris, New York and Milan—is changing its original boundaries. Humanity is too rich, heterogeneous, multicultural and dynamic to center its attention exclusively on these four cities. While we continue to view these places as the neuralgic centers of fashion, we are increasingly paying attention to designs coming out of different parts of the world, ones that promise to explode the panorama of international fashion in the years ahead.

This is the idea on which *Atlas of Fashion Designers* is based: the importance of looking beyond the epicenters of fashion, yet without losing sight of them. It represents a way of evolving in a diverse, increasingly connected world, one in which a 180-degree turn is expected in the new millennium.

In contrast to previous years, the most important international catwalks are beginning to be dotted with the work of designers of diverse origins: Russians, Indians, Brazilians, Poles, Chinese, Pakistanis, Israelis, Ghanaians, South Africans… This shift is a reflection of the new millennium, one characterized by a melting pot of cultures that wish to express and reassert their identity in an increasingly globalized world.

The principal aim of this book is to demonstrate the heterogeneous nature of current fashion, fashion that transcends frontiers as the only mode of growing and renovating itself in order to avoid becoming obsolete, fashion that keeps in step with the signs and symbols that define our times. Identity, globalization, place, hybridization, sustainability, innovation, research, luxury, and new systems of productions, all linked to craftsmanship and fair trade, form the centerpiece of the work of designers who articulate this new conception of identity in the twenty-first century, one with local roots yet a global projection.

Such is the case of Brazilian designer Isabela Capeto, whose work is characterized by its high level of social commitment and a warm, indigenous craftsmanship marketed successfully throughout the world. This is also true of Indian designer Manish Arora, who has ably transported his singular aesthetic to Western markets, ones fascinated by the exuberant richness of his culture. These examples are no accident, as India and Brazil, along with Russian and China (the so-called BRIC nations), are countries in full economic expansion

Photography courtesy of Nina Donis

that are penetrating and taking positions in the world of fashion, with designers such as the abovementioned Manish Arora and Isabela Capeto, as well as Ashish Gupta in India; Anunciação and Karlla Girotto in Brazil; Nina Donis, Denis Simachev, Alena Akhmadullina and Igor Chapurin in Russia; and Blanc de Chine in China.

Along this same line of vindicating one's own identity, designers are also emerging who delve into their own culture and proudly export the best of their tradition in the form of luxury brands, such as South African label Sun Goddess and the Chinese brand Blanc de Chine. Others fight to keep haute couture out in front, such as renowned brands like Viktor & Rolf, Alber Elbaz for Lanvin, Karl Lagerfeld for Chanel, or the recently arrived Spaniard to Parisian haute couture, Josep Font.

Textile research and the forging of new paths also represent the spearhead of current fashion. This can be seen in the work of Helen Storey of Great Britain, whose highly original way of fusing the worlds of science and fashion is carried out through an eponymous foundation, as well as in the work of designers finding alternatives to textiles in recycled garments, such as New Yorker Susan Cianciolo, Brazilian Karlla Girotto, and the inimitable Maison Martin Margiela, whose "Artisanal" line attempts to inject new life into obsolete garments and objects.

In *Atlas of Fashion Designers*, men's fashion takes root within a predominantly feminine panorama, redefining itself without casting aside its traditional character through displays of exquisite skill and mastery of classical tailoring. British Timothy Everest and Neil Barrett, North Americans Thom Browne and Craig Robinson, Dutch of Hindu origin Jeroen van Tuyl, and Ghanaian Joe Casely-Hayford are some of the designers who, from an innovative perspective, view the masculine wardrobe with a tailor's eyes.

Sixty-nine designers of thirty-two different nationalities, all working in fashion from diverse perspectives, places, cultures, identities, techniques and philosophies, make up the map of current fashion presented in this book, one in which the reader will find not every new designer out there, but will encounter every one that is changing the face of fashion today.

Addy van den Krommenacker

Photography by Jeroen Snijders

Addy van den Krommenacker

The fashion shows of designer Addy van den Krommenacker exude pure classical cinema. Kim Novak, Veronica Lake and Joan Crawford could easily choose his elegant and refined pearl satin dresses for having a gin fizz in any cocktail bar. If there is something that this Dutch designer knows how to do with his mastery, it is recreating the elegance of the golden age of Hollywood and making it available to today's woman.

His creations, elegant and distinguished with precise patterns, tailored waists and a studied hang, envelop the delicate figure of a woman who wishes to be elegant, special and breathtakingly feminine with care and brilliantly luxurious materials, recovering the glamour of 50s and 60s cinema.

In a shifting and increasingly androgynous aesthetic universe, one in which the reinterpretation of femininity is at the forefront, Addy van den Krommenacker looks backward in order to recover the mysterious women reflected so well in the cinema of previous decades.

It is no surprise, then, that his unabashed objective is for today's woman to feel like a princess, an aim that can be felt in each pleat and every hang of his dresses. In the game of seduction that he proposes, the women he dresses need only show up to draw attention to themselves, to make the slightest gesture to cause a sensation wherever they go.

Photography by Jeroen Snijders

Photography by Jeroen Snijders

The designs of Addy van den Krommenacker are conceived for standing out on the red carpet, due to their delicacy, feminine forms, and, more than anything, the fact that the Dutch designer knows better than anyone else the meaning of the word "elegance" linked to the most cinematographic glamour.

Addy van den Krommenacker

Photography by Jeroen Snijders

- What inspires you?

My inspirations are movie stars throughout the decades. Women are so elegant in the movies of the 50s and 60s. I like to make clothes with the area of those times and the comfort of today.

- What is your dream as a designer?

My dream is that women all over the world feel like princesses in my clothes and are happy that they bought a dress from my collection.

- What has been the most important achievement of your career?

The most important achievement is my prize of best foreign designer at the Look of the Year event in Italy.

- How important are trends?

Trends are important, but I like to make clothes that are timeless, which you still can wear whenever you want to. On the other hand, I like to dress stars in trendy clothes of mine.

- What does fashion reflect in the twenty-first century?

Fashion these days is a combination of the 50s and the 80s. Clothes nowadays need to be comfortable and practical while retaining the glamour of the new area.

- What book would you recommend to every fashion designer?

The book I would recommend is the history of Balenciaga.

Addy van den Krommenacker

Verwersstraat 79

5211 HV 's–Hertogenbosch

The Netherlands

www.addyvandenkrommenacker.nl

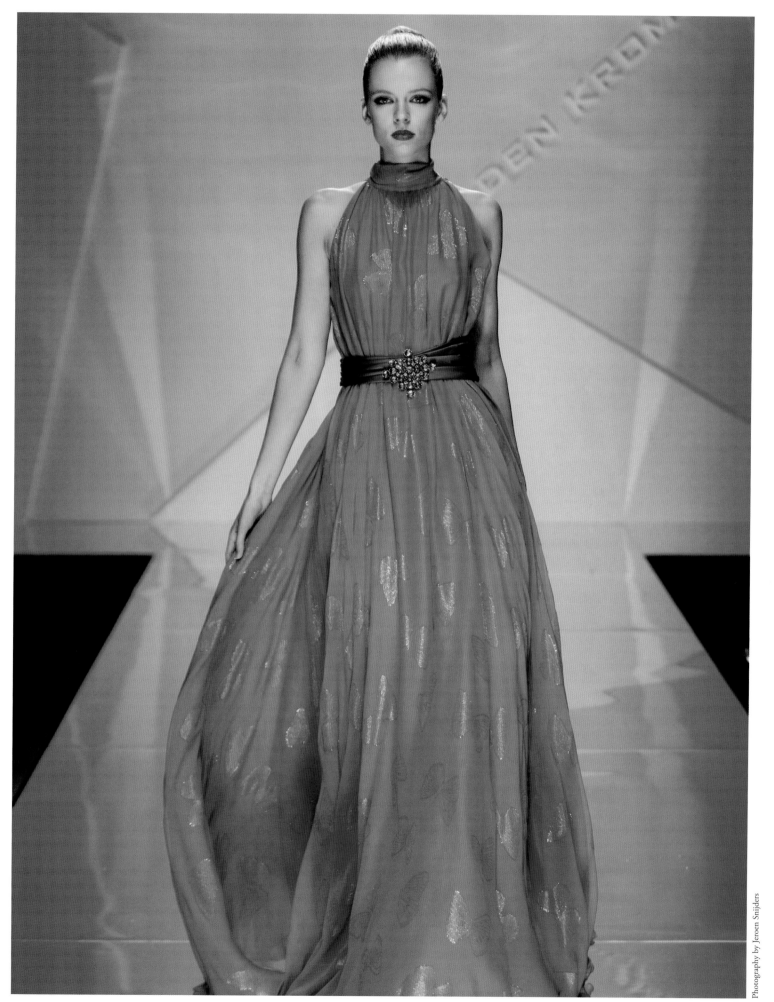

15

Addy van den Krommenacker

Photography by Jeroen Snijders

Addy van den Krommenacker

Photography by Jeroen Snijders

Photography by Jeroen Snijders

The principal fabrics of this Spring/
Summer 2008 collection were
pure silk, organdy, brocades, and
silk chiffon, which along with the
volumes and pleats of dresses proved
triumphant on Rome's Haute Couture
catwalk.

© Photography by Stéphane Gallois

18
Alber Elbaz (Lanvin)

Alber Elbaz (Lanvin)

At the age of twenty-five and with 800 euros in his pocket, Alber Elbaz packs his bags and sets off to New York to seek his fortune. In 2007, he appears in *Time* magazine as one of the 100 most influential people in the world. So far, there's nothing so odd about this: the typical story of a hardened man who's had enough, drops everything in pursuit of a dream and attains it. What is not common about it, however, is that Alber is one of the most beloved professionals in the field of fashion. His earns elicit swarms of praise not only for his creations but for the designer himself. The creative passion he invests in his garments is also shared with his admirers and the people he works with.

He began his career with a small fashion company. Later, he came into contact with Geoffrey Beane, who taught him the rules of tailoring which would make him the refined and meticulous designer he is today. In 1997, he began working with Guy Laroche and subsequently worked with Yves Saint Laurent on the design of his pret-a-porter collection, a project in which demonstrated the depth of his dedication and affection in spectacularly realized work. Some time after, Alber distanced himself from the project, in what he himself has described as an emotionally traumatic separation, given that it involved the splitting up of a group, of a family. He then moved on to Lanvin. Entering this company was, for him, the equivalent of inheriting a noble title, an arrival to an established institution where he has not only found a home, but has elevated the legendary house to an even higher place in the fashion firmament. All of this is the result of lavish self-expression in the form of unrepentant volumes and pleats and garments sculpted by the air. An artist in a joyful reencounter with his universe. Alber Elbaz: a designer whose creations are as moving as the man himself.

Photography by David Sims

Alber Elbaz (Lanvin)

© Lanvin

With characteristic mastery, Alber
Elbaz offered a Spring/Summer 2008-
2009 collection charged with color,
fluid textures and spherical forms. In
these images, we find two cocktail
dresses in electric colors of brilliant
satin.

© Lanvin

- What inspires you?

Everything inspires me: light, emotions, my neighbors…

- What is your dream as a designer?

Having more time. I would like to push back the limits of each day.

- What has been the most important achievement of your career?

My wedding day with Lanvin in 2001.

- How important are trends?

My philosophy aims to make women beautiful, no matter the trends.

- Fashion has always reflected a certain era. What does fashion reflect in the twenty-first century?

It reflects a time of technique and technology, where we use the past in a modern way.

- What book would you recommend to every fashion designer?

Lanvin book by Rizzoli Publications, or the work of Jeanne Lanvin revealed in broad daylight.

Alber Elbaz (Lanvin)
15, rue du Faubourg Saint-Honoré
75008 Paris
France
www.lanvin.com

23
Alber Elbaz (Lanvin)

© Lanvin

Photography courtesy of Alena Akhmadullina

Alena Akhmadullina

In just one glance, an anthropologist attending an Alena Akhmadullina show could gather synthetic information about the historical and cultural legacy of Russia in recent times. In her collections, fragments of Russian iconography succeed one another as if they were archeological vestiges of another time.

Russian constructivism, the Cossack and military look, and the aesthetic influence of the painter Tamara de Lempicka are some of the influences at work in her creations, which consist of a mosaic of aspects astutely reinterpreted and assimilated with pride and elegance.

It would seem that a young woman born in the Leningradsky Region with dreams of becoming a designer would be tempted to abandon her roots and follow the guidelines set by the icons of fashion in New York, Paris, Milan, and Britain. Alena, however, has remained true to herself, presenting her art just as it is. And many are the prizes she has earned for exhibiting this respect toward herself, this dignified attitude. Since graduating from the State University of Technology and Design in St. Petersburg, she has received a slew of important awards, including the best designer at Moscow's Dress of the Year in 1999 and, in 2000, the Smirnoff International Prize for Design.

And the fact is Alena remains original while simultaneously embracing the past, innovative in salvaging what is obsolete, unique and unparalleled in immersing herself in the collective iconography of her homeland. For this reason, she is considered one of the most important discoveries in Russian design of recent times.

Photography courtesy of Alena Akhmadullina

Photography courtesy of Alena Akhmadullina

The aesthetic of the Russian designer's Fall/Winter 2007–2008 collection takes inspiration in a nineteenth-century photography salon: women dressed in masculine suit jackets as a symbol of the incipient women's liberation.

Photography courtesy of Alena Akhmadullina

27
Alena Akhmadullina

- What inspires you?

Plentiful Russian culture and art inspire me in the creation of my collections. For instance, I'm interested in the history of the Russian czars. The mystique of both Russian customs and literature appeal to me. I mean various mystifications, charming transformations and dialogue with natural power, as well. In clothes, it can be expressed by using plenty of prints or by the presence of unique, concealed details.

- What is your dream as a designer?

To answer the purposes of the brand's business context, possessing immaculate creative latitude. For any designer, reaching such harmony is the highest stage of professionalism. You are creating a collection the way buyers want it, and it is moving successfully.

- What has been the most important achievement of your career?

Our brand develops step by step, and every step is an achievement. A recent success was the active creation of the brand's team, consisting of very talented, unique people. They make my job a work of art. Our relationship and cooperation is very interesting, and I'm sure that very soon it will be reflected in the brand itself.

- How important are trends?

Fashion is a current art, which is why trends are very important. In the luxury segment, a brand's ability to produce trends and to be in phase with other designers' ideas brings not only moral and creative satisfaction, but also impressive figures in the profits column.

- Fashion has always reflected a certain era. What does fashion reflect in the twenty-first century?

Fashion cannot but retreat to background experience. And it is endless. Just as fashion's visualization of the future is most often expressed in the use of glossy materials, minimalist forms and space technologies. That is why designers often return to past decades, established styles and previous streams of art when creating a collection. Such nostalgia always cuts to the client's heart, so it is very pleasant to work with. Although, using different vintage forms and transforming them in the right way, it is possible to read a fashion of futurity.

- What book would you recommend to every fashion designer?

The books of Alexandr Vasiliev are the most delicate, elegant and exact research of fashion history. All of these publications are filled not only with unique photo materials, but also with very deep analysis of everything in the fashion industry during a given time slot.

Alena Akhmadullina
Rochdelsky, 15
123022 Moscow
Russia
www.alenaakhmadullina.com

Alena Akhmadullina

Photography courtesy of Alena Akhmadullina

Photography courtesy of Alena Akhmadullina

In this Spring/Summer 2007 collection, Alena Akhmadullina delved into her past to give us garments in white tones inspired by the vertical static dresses of cutout dolls, as if they attached to the body thanks to a little tab.

Photography courtesy of Alena Akhmadullina

Sketch courtesy of Alena Akhmadullina

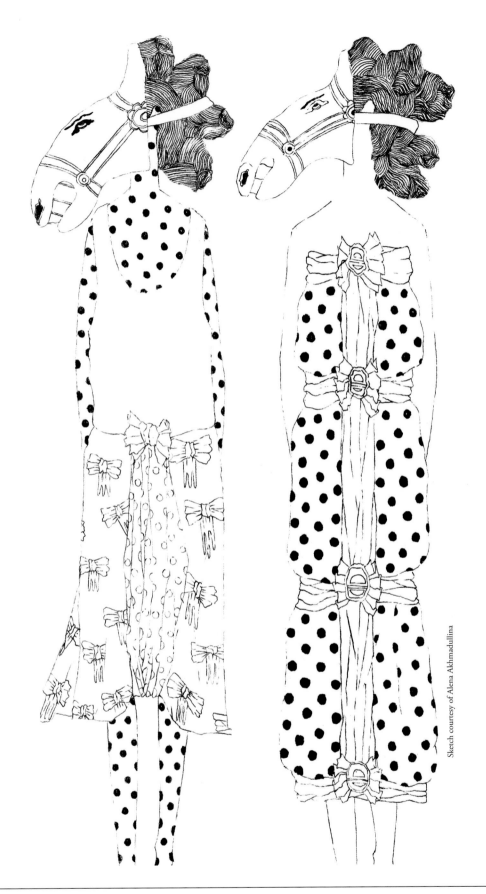

Sketch courtesy of Alena Akhmadullina

In these sketches from the Spring/Summer 2006 collection, Alena returns to one of her most common sources of inspiration: Russian folklore, in which it is customary to dress up as animals in popular celebrations, as these drawings of a horse's head on a human body demonstrate.

Photography by Dan Martensen

Alexander Wang

If at first glance anything calls attention to Alexander Wang, it would be his youth. At just twenty-three, he has already become one of the designers that young Americans adore most. This is due in large part to his ability to give his garments that insouciant yet elegant urban look that so fascinates Americans, one not everyone knows how to carry off with such skill and expertise. This, alongside a style founded on the juxtaposition of elements (good and bad taste, the 80s and current trends, the luxurious and the basic, etc.), has given Wang's creations an unusual identity that adapts very well to current preferences.

His designs are cherished by urban women with a rebellious bent, in search of comfortable garments with a flawless cut and the refined silhouettes of fashion that emerges from the street. This makes perfect sense, given his youth and restlessness. He is both an observer of and participant in the germination of these street trends, as well as the first to capture and reproduce them in the form of collections. An example of this is his Spring/Summer 2008 collection, which offered an unconventional reading of 80s fashion filtered through the lens of the movie *Working Girl*, exploring the feminine work wardrobe and reinterpreting it for current times.

Alexander was born in California in the heart of a Chinese-American family. When he was eighteen, he decided to leave San Francisco and move to New York to study at the Parsons School of Design. In a short time, he has traveled an impressively long road. Marc Jacobs and Derek Lam are some of the brands he has worked for, and still under twenty-five, he is now presenting his seventh collection. In short, he is a true prodigy of fashion.

Photography by Dan Martensen

Spring/Summer 2008 collection for
women looking for comfort, freshness
and the opportunity to explore the chicest
side of their nature. Above, oversize
garments combined with mini shorts
or drainpipe trousers represented some
of Alexander's most striking designs.

Photographies by Dan Martensen

Alexander Wang

Photography by Dan Martensen

- What inspires you?

Inspiration usually doesn't stray too far from home. It's my friends, the streets, art and music. I try not to push too hard to find inspiration, because it's usually right under my nose.

- What is your dream as a designer?

To change the way people perceive what is acceptable for red carpet fashion and to create a lifestyle that people can adapt to and feel comfortable in.

- What has been the most important achievement of your career?

To actually be sold in stores is thrilling, and so is having an amazing team working with me.

- How important are trends?

Not important at all. A trend means you are conforming, and that's not what my brand is about.

- Fashion has always reflected a certain era. What does fashion reflect in the twenty-first century?

For me, it's individuality and comfort.

- The book you would recommend to every fashion designer is...

Atlas of Fashion Designers.

Alexander Wang
386 Broadway, 3rd floor
New York, NY 10013
United States
www.alexanderwang.com

Photography by Dan Martensen

Alexandra Moura

© Rui Vasco/courtesy of Moda Lisboa

Alexandra Moura

Alexandra's designs evoke a somber, exhausted landscape; a misty, futuristic panorama populated by garments with pleats and knots that intersect to form organic fabrics; a second skin, melancholy yet comfortable, created out of elegant materials and pale colors that warmly embrace and shield the body.

Alexandra was born in Lisbon, where she received her training as a designer. It is easy to appreciate the nostalgic atmosphere of the city in her work. Nonetheless, her creations do not represent a yearning for the past; retro references are few and far between, and there is an absence of sentimental longing for times past and traditional Portuguese fado music. Instead, an existential sadness sets its gaze on the near future. For this reason, the designer dresses artists that embody the new, modern, sophisticated spirit of Lisbon such as Madredeus lead singer Teresa Salgueiro. The rough sophistication of her garments could very well be employed in the recreation of a science fiction movie, her designs and colors reminiscent of the sober futurism of *Mad Max* and *Blade Runner*. An elegant, disaffected look. Simple, comfortable, and the very opposite of ornate.

Since 2001, Alexandra's career has drawn attention to itself through the designer's participation in numerous events and projects. Her collections are shown twice a year during Lisbon Fashion Week, and her designs have appeared at various European events such as the Biennale Internationale du Design in Saint Étienne, Bread and Butter in Barcelona, and the 12th Belgrade Fashion Week. With the same flexibility characteristic of her work, Alexandra continues to carve out a place for herself in the world of international fashion, exhibiting her Portuguese spirit by reinventing a Lisbon of the future.

Photography by Diana Dias

© Rui Vasco/courtesy of Moda Lisboa

Reflecting her exhaustive study of the human body, the Lisboan designer presents this Fall/Winter 2007–2008 collection based on the structures of organic tissues like muscle, tendons and cartilage.

© Rui Vasco/courtesy of Moda Lisboa

- What inspires you?

A photo, a person, an object, a sensation, a feeling. Everything that is beautiful through my eyes, everything that has the capability to put me in another world, another dimension, everything that makes me dream and gives me the power to have ideas.

- What is your dream as a designer?

The constant challenge of creating and achieving ideas. It is, no doubt, the designer's dream.

- What has been the most important achievement of your career?

My main achievement is the fact that I have a company that produces and sells my ideas.

- How important are trends?

Trends are important mainly because of information and the constant updates on the times we are living. It is important to look for the trends, but they are just information. With my creations, I don't follow trends; I just follow ideas and concepts, which I explore until exhaustion, finally arriving at the collection.

- Fashion has always reflected a certain era. What does fashion reflect in the twenty-first century?

It is a reflection of the fusion of several eras in a single moment, the fusion of various criticisms and analyses of different states of mind. It has all become a special, singular twenty-first century fashion.

- What book would you recommend to every fashion designer?

Histoires de la mode, written by Didier Grumbach.

Alexandra Moura
Rua Latino Coelho, 33, 1º esq.
1050-132 Lisbon
Portugal
www.alexandramoura.com

Alexandra Moura

© Rui Vasco/courtesy of Moda Lisboa

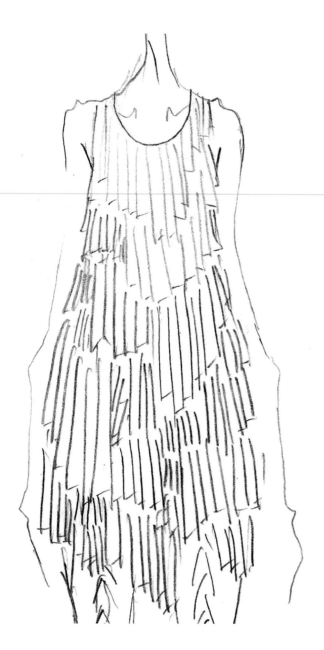

Sketch courtesy of Alexandra Moura

Illustrations by Alexandra Moura for
the Fall/Winter 2007-2008 season.
Knots, interlaced fabrics of different
textures, and cream colors were the
principal actors in this collection.

Alexandra Moura

© Rui Vasco/courtesy of Moda Lisboa

Sketch courtesy of Alexandra Moura

Sketches and compositions made from
remnants and different accessories
is the starting point for the singular
collections with which Alexandra
shakes up fashion runways.

4

CANADAS

Braco

MALHA JAPONESA BRANCA

CINTO (tecidos)
brilho
+
Musseline
(COMO OS DE INVERNO

Malha

5

TUDO Malha

Sketch courtesy of Alexandra Moura

Ángel Sánchez

Photography by Dan & Corina Lecca

Ángel Sánchez

Ángel Sánchez gladly entered the family business, a sewing shop in Venezuela specializing in customized work, where he soaked up fashion over the years among the sewing machines and scissors. Time and other interests, however, caused his initial dream to gradually fade, and he ended up enrolling as an architecture student at Universidad Simón Bolivar in Caracas. Ángel's architectural studies provided him with the additional tools he needed to arrive at the profession he finally opted for: that of fashion designer. With this idea in mind and a head full of doubts, he thus decided to devote himself to fashion.

In 1995, Ángel opened his own showroom in New York. That same year, the coronation of a Miss Venezuela dressed in one of his garments made it clear to him that he had been born to make dresses for the most beautiful women on the planet. His garments are an architecturally immaculate armature conceived to emphasize femininity with elegance. Made with a meticulous attention to detail, his light, vaporous designs extol the figure of a harmoniously proportioned woman.

As Karl Lagerfeld and Cavalli did for H&M, Ángel has designed a collection for the Venezuelan chain Beco, in what seems to represent an evolution from the most refined haute couture to a more elaborate and elegant pret-a-porter for everyday wear.

The trajectory of this great master has extended beyond the frontiers of his native Venezuela, and he is currently one of the most coveted designers for the biggest stars in Hollywood. And the fact is that few are able to build dreams on a single pattern.

Photography by Anibal Mestre

To the right, a black silk tulle cocktail dress. Over it, tulle body embroidered in small antique silver pieces. To the left, deep blue silk chiffon dress. All belong to the 2008 "Evening Resort" collection.

Photography by Dan & Corina Lecca

Photography by Dan & Corina Lecca

- What inspires you?

In my work, you find nostalgia and modernity existing alongside each other. Nostalgia comes from my childhood fascination with the cinematography of the 50s, but the simple lines are the result of my training as an architect.

As an architect, each design begins with a drawing, but it's the construction and the way a dress gets assembled that interests me most—achieving the right proportion and hang, and without being a minimalist, trying to economize when it comes to ornamentation and different purposes in a single design.

The romantic and Latin side is also very present. I'm seduced by the drama and impact a design can generate, and I'm fascinated by that almost forgotten sense of elegance and glamour, which is why I always work with classical figures, although I reinterpret them, giving them a subtly modern and unexpected touch.

- What is your dream as a designer?

Like any designer, I have to admit that I want international recognition and to grow and expand in terms of offers and products, but I don't dream of inspiring a revolution with my work. The truth is, I only try to use fashion as a way of expressing myself, and for me it would be a great achievement to continue feeling the intimate and immediate satisfaction that I've always felt with my work and to enjoy being acknowledged for it along the way, which would give me the necessary resources and strength to express my ideas in a more definitive way.

- What has been the most important achievement of your career?

My wisest decision was made just as I was enjoying my best professional moment in my country. It was having taken the risk and having had the courage to move beyond the boundaries of my own success and face an international competition. After that, my wisest move was being able to persevere and survive until I'd made a name for myself, even if just a small one, in a business as competitive as this one.

- How important are trends?

I make use of trends as a way of ensuring that my own work evolves and doesn't grow old and repeat itself.

- Fashion has always reflected a certain era. What does fashion reflect in the twenty-first century?
Accessibility and freedom.

- What book would you recommend to every fashion designer?
A biography of Cristobal Balenciaga. It could be *Cristóbal Balenciaga* by Lesley Ellis Miller (1993).

Ángel Sánchez
148 West 37th Street, 7th floor
New York, NY 10018
United States
www.angelsanchezusa.com

Photography courtesy of Ángel Sánchez

Angel Sanche

Angel S

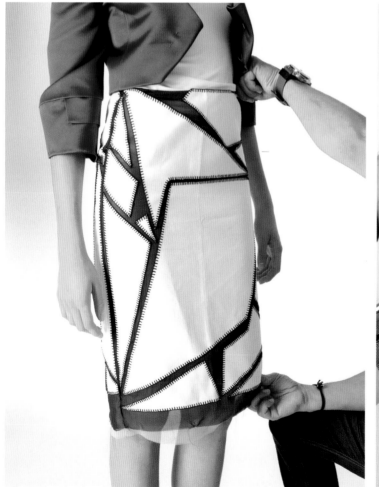

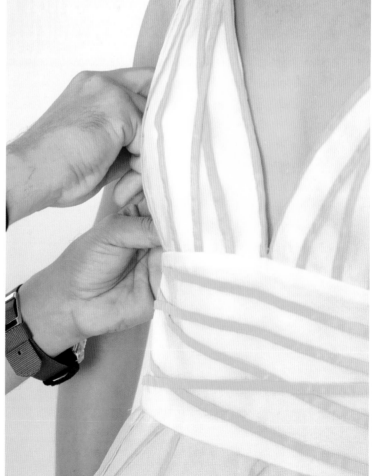

Photographies by Dana Meilijson

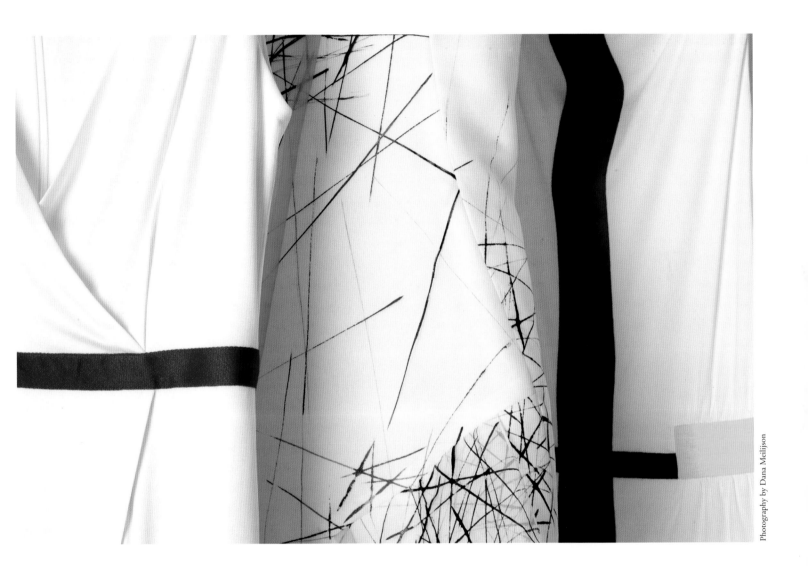

Photography by Dana Meilijson

Trained in architecture, Ángel Sánchez
resorts constantly to cultural and
academic references in his work, as in
the Spring/Summer 2008 collection,
the creative process of which can been
seen in these images.

Photography by Rogério Mesquita/styling by Greisson Albuquerque/model: Taísa Maciel

Anunciação

Appreciating the beauty of the work of María Elvira Crosara requires only a glance. But if you move a little closer, you will see that these garments are also the result of the slow sedimentation of cultures. The dresses, kimonos and shirts from Anunciação's latest collection emerge from the confluence of an Italian artistic training and the raw force of Rio de Janeiro, all of it awash in the aesthetic imaginings of a Colombian illustrator with undeniable Japanese influences.

María Elvira was raised in Goiás among table linens, embroidery and the meticulously crafted curtains of local artisans. Before long, she decided to follow her own passions, traveling to Florence to study jewelry design at the Italian School of Fashion Design. She later completed this training with classes in fashion design at Universidade Federal in Goiás.

In 2003, without much pomp, the company Anunciação was born. This gave free rein to the artist's evocative and unusual aesthetic universe. With a certain collector's spirit, her childhood memories are brought forth, in addition to a taste for embroidery, a joyful tribute to nature and life inherent in all her creations, and a deep respect for craftsmanship, which is reflected in the names of the individuals that hand-embroider her designs.

Festive colors and the pagan tropics imbue the work of Anunciação, printed on an exquisite, meticulous cut that transmits fresh and subtle sensuality. All of this is the result of the vision of an extremely talented designer who is able to articulate her unique perspective with rare balance and immaculate taste.

Photography by Rogério Mesquita

Illustration by Catalina Estrada

Illustrations by Colombian illustrator
Catalina Estrada in which the artist
establishes a nexus between her
own imagination and the world of
Anunciação. To the right, two designs
with prints by the artist from the
Spring/Summer 2008 collection.

60
Anunciação

Photographs by Rogério Mesquita/styling by Greisson Albuquerque/model: Taísa Maciel

- What inspires you?

My creations start with events from daily life, a dreamlike process. For example, when I started drawing the Summer 2007 collection, I saw an image of women from an African tribe standing in line, waiting in silence to receive medical aid. I was very moved to see them wearing such wonderfully elaborated, colorful garments while surrounded by such harshness. It was a moment where beauty beat misery.

- What is your dream as a designer?

The history of art is the history of humanity's quest for its essence. The act of creation is essentially human, and whenever I see the wonderful things we humans make, I feel like contributing toward making the world a more pleasant place.

- What has been the most important achievement of your career?

It is important to me to see people combining my creations in their own personal way and wearing the clothes that pleases them most. I love to see each person develop his or her own style.

- How important are trends?

I believe one's particular level of acceptance of trends is related to one's sense of self-identification with them. This feeling may be strong or weak, depending on one's personal life experiences and culture. It is important to know the difference between a product that you can develop a personal relationship with and a product that is the result of trend research. I believe in timeless design that is not determined by seasons or trends.

- Fashion has always reflected a certain era. What does fashion reflect in the twenty-first century?

The twenty-first century is a time of relativity. We live in societies that have broken many rules, and at times we are lost, without limits. We are supplied with a great amount of information, but that does not assure us the creation of something interesting. We can create nothing, a mix of meaningless things, or something that reflects a particular arrangement. I don't seek originality or art; I just want to do my best at my work!

- What book would you recommend to every fashion designer?

The Guatemala Rainbow (photographs by Gianni Vecchiato). I especially like anthropology books, because they present you with the beliefs and customs of a people, which reflect on the design of their daily objects and artifacts. This is the difference between creating only through aesthetic references and creating with the support of history as inspiration.

Anunciação
Rua Oscar Freire, 540
01426-000 São Paulo, SP
Brazil
www.anunciacao.com

Anunciação

Illustration by Catalina Estrada

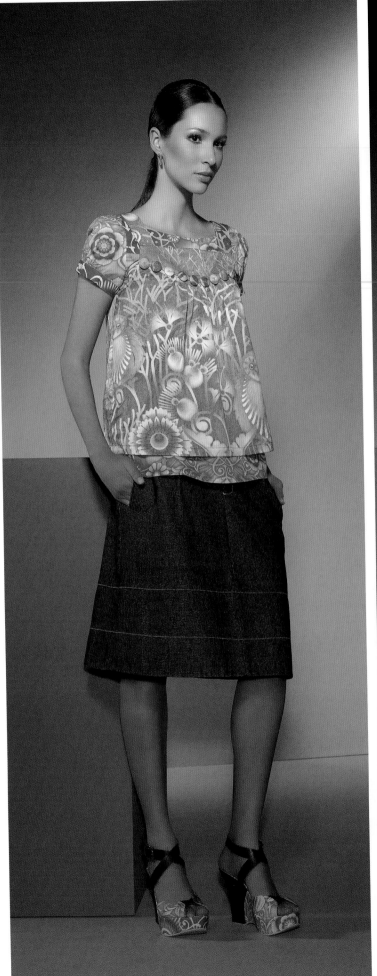

Photographs by Rogério Mesquita/styling by Greisson Albuquerque/model: Taisa Maciel

Illustration by Catalina Estrada

Anunciação and Catalina Estrada
join forces to create prints for shirts,
T-shirts, dresses, skirts, and even
sandals, as well as other accessories
charged with exoticism, naturalness
and mystery.

Illustration by Sonia Paiva

With its marked coloristic, upbeat
character, along with a healthy dose of
tropicalism, the Anunciação label continues
to evolve in the direction originally charted
by the designer, with forays at times into
more naïve terrain, as demonstrated by the
designs on these pages.

Photographs by Rogério Mesquita/styling by Greisson Albuquerque/model: Taísa Maciel

Ashish

Ashish's beginnings are bound to a kind of journey of initiation between fate and providence, a tumultuous swinging back and forth that guided the bright star of this young designer at the outset of his career. When Ashish completed his master's degree at prestigious Central Saint Martins, he gathered up all of his work and set off to Paris to seek his fortune. Before even emerging from the Gare du Nord train station, however, his portfolio had been robbed. Penniless, he was forced to return to his native India. There, and with little pretense, he created a small collection with which he would return to London. As fate would have it, a friend photographed wearing one of his jackets brought more attention to Ashish's work than a mass mailing to practically all the fashion agencies in town.

As a result of this stroke of random good fortune, Ashish made a name for himself. It is for this reason that the Indian designer embraces providential changes, in what he considers a philosophy of life: from the bad something good can emerge; from the small, something grand. In this same spirit, he embraces the liberty and freshness of a society without castes, the multiracial, effervescent spirit of the London of the 70s: the eternal icon of cultural freedom.

Ashish recreates this period with sparkling sequined mini dresses combined with colored stockings sheathed in lace, superimpositions, fluorine colors, sheen, paillet, and precious stones—a genuine stardust worn by Madonna, Goldfrapp and other musical luminaries at one time or another. Indeed, the glorious fusion of high culture and mass culture, the combination of yin and yang, is what has made this designer one of the great new promises of London Fashion Week.

Photography by Will Sanders

Photography by Will Sanders/make up by Shama/hair by Tom Kembery/model: Aisha

Photography by Will Sanders/make up by Shama/hair by Tom Kembery/model: Nadja B

To the left, a dress from the Fall/
Winter 2007–2008 collection. To
the right, shorts and patterned shirts
from the Spring/Summer 2007
collection that represent the designer's
characteristic style: a combination of
sexy, glamorous and casual.

- What inspires you?

Lots of different things are inspiring. It could be a film I've watched or a book I'm reading. Friends are inspiring, as is the way people dress in the street. I also find travel very inspiring. And I am obsessed with color and light—I never met a sequin I didn't like!

- What is your dream as a designer?

To be able to continue to make a living from doing what I love doing.

- What has been the most important achievement of your career?

I think it's really thrilling when I see a stranger wearing one of my designs.

- How important are trends?

I don't really look at trends. I prefer to go with my instinct for what feels right at the moment.

- Fashion has always reflected a certain era. What does fashion reflect in the twenty-first century?

Fashion is now completely celebrity-obsessed and moves at an incredibly fast pace. The boundary between high fashion and high street has become increasingly blurry. Also, Western fashion is becoming more and more international; very few parts of the globe have not been permeated by cheap, mass-manufactured Western clothing, which is mainly manufactured in the developing world.

- What book would you recommend to every fashion designer?

D.V., by Diana Vreeland.

Ashish
25B Kempe Road
London NW6 6SP
United Kingdom
www.ashish.co.uk

Photography by Will Sanders/make up by Shama/hair by Tom Kembery/model: Nadja B

Both images show one of the star garments from the Fall/Winter 2007–2008 collection: a quilted coat of bright fabric with a large bow at the waist that evokes an aesthetic somewhere between kitsch and the utmost glitter of disco.

Photography by Will Sanders/make up by Shama/hair by Tom Kembery/model: Nadja B

Photography by Will Sanders/make up by Shama/hair by Tom Kembery/model: Nadja B

Ashish

Avsh Alom Gur

Photography by Ian Gillett

Avsh Alom Gur

For a designer with clear ideas, working for another label can be a genuine torture. And this tends to be the case with all creators in the making: first, you must cloak yourself in the identities of others and then, little by little, come up with ideas that allow you to express yourself. This is how Avsh Alom Gur began his career, holding different positions and fulfilling a variety of responsibilities at other labels (Donna Karan, Roberto Cavalli and Chloé, among others) before creating his own collections.

Still, the uncomfortable predicament of not being able to express oneself was not completely alien to Avsh. This Israeli-born designer, who studied in London and considers himself British, learned early on that being oneself requires the determination to move beyond one's cultural origins, not to mention the courage to combine remnants from here and there in the creation of a suit in step with current fashion.

The work of Avsh demonstrates a great capacity for combining global cultural references and traditional techniques from many different places. Urban, natural, traditional, modern—all serve as a foundation for developing his creations. In his own words: "Everything, everywhere, all the time."

The mix of the possible and the probable—such as his Spring/Summer 2007 collection in which a woman abandoned on a futuristic deserted island is surrounded by fishnets, chiffons, caftans and beach wraps printed by textile designer Daniel Rayne—represents a bold aesthetic exercise, a study of the artistic possibilities available to fashion, the work, in short, of a designer for whom limitations are only a matter of choice.

Photography by Vanessa Ellis

Sketches courtesy of Avsh Alom Gur

The Israeli designer utilized a palette of ochre colors for his Fall/Winter 2006–2007 collection. Above, sketches from this collection. To the right, two designs that combine diverse materials, such as delicate silk with tough cotton in tatters.

Photographies by Ian Gillett

79
Avsh Alom Gur

- What inspires you?

Anything and everything from my daily vision! I can usually find something unique and beautiful in what others might think of as mess or dirt.

- What is your dream as a designer?

To be able to work in what I love doing and be lucky to be enough for people to appreciate it.

- What has been the most important achievement of your career?

Being able to sustain an independent, highly creative fashion label while working with a team of incredible, talented, young individuals.

- How important are trends?

Not important at all for the certain fashion and level at which I'm operating. It's extremely important and fundamental for high street fashion.

- Fashion has always reflected a certain era. What does fashion reflect in the twenty-first century?

Freedom of liberating your soul and following your gut feeling in the way we dress.

- The book you would recommend to every fashion designer is...

Farm, by Jackie Nickerson.

Avsh Alom Gur

158 Milligan Street

London E14 8AS

United Kingdom

www.avshalomgur.com

Sketch courtesy of Avsh Alom Gur

Avsh Alom Gur

Sketches courtesy of Avsh Alom Gur

Sketches from various seasons and images from the Spring/Summer 2006 and Spring/Summer 2007 collections. The prints on the designs reflect the interest of Avsh Alom Gur in arts and crafts and ethnic motifs.

Photography by Vanessa Ellis

Photography by Ian Gillett

Photography courtesy of Avsh Alom

Collage from the Spring/Summer
2007 collection and a design from the
same season, both of which embody
the designer's preference for pastel
colors and the fusion of the apparently
unconnected, such as cotton jewelry.

Photography by Ian Gillett

Photography by Niall McInerney

A conciliatory vision of East and West exists within the designer, one that manifests itself quite clearly in his collections alongside an uncanny ability for reconciling opposites: luxury/poverty, tradition/avant-garde…

Avsh Alom Gur

Photography by Niall McInerney

Photography by Fernanda Calfat

Basso & Brooke

From Rio de Janeiro designer Bruno Basso and English illustrator Christopher Brooke comes Basso & Brooke, one of the most renowned and leading companies of the London avant-garde. Born in Santos, Brazil, Bruno Basso soon began to develop a career in the art world as a producer, organizer, and art director. Christopher Brooke studied at Central Saint Martins, where he distinguished himself by graduating with honors in his major. A year later, he was assisting Joe Casely-Hayford. It was at this time when, fortunately, he ran into Bruno Basso.

The encounter between these two talents has been the most difficult part of both of their artistic careers, for once the creative union of Basso & Brooke was consummated, success has been nonstop. In 2004, their work earned the prestigious London Fashion Fringe award thanks to a collection overflowing with sensuality. Their Fall/Winter 2004–2005 collection was acquired by New York's Metropolitan Museum of Art, and the multinational group Aeffe banked on their rare talent along with that of designers of the caliber of Alberta Ferretti, Moschino, and Gaultier.

The success of Basso & Brooke attests to its creators' great skill in the realization of their ideas. Cutting and printing work is done at the same time, which results in compact garments that explore the graphic and pastel aesthetics of the 80s, as well as art nouveau. Basso & Brooke is a living example of strength in numbers, of the fact that the fusion of two nationalities and two distinct careers can result in work of unbounded quality. It's no surprise, then, that these two designers represent one of the most refreshing and innovative promises on the current fashion scene.

Photography courtesy of Basso & Brooke

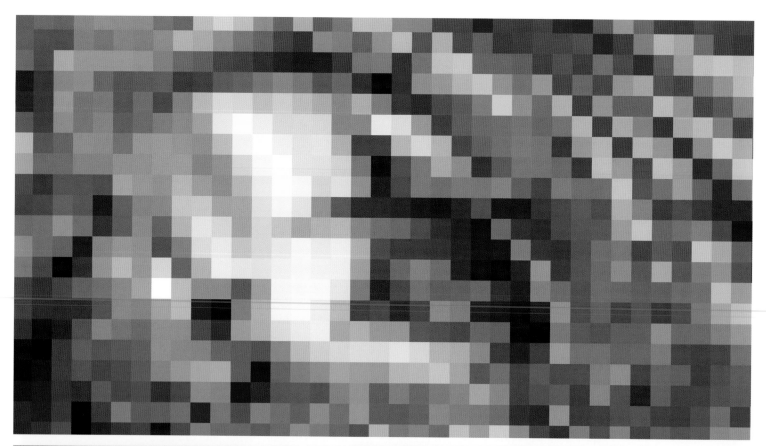

Sketches courtesy of Basso & Brooke

To the left, drawings by Christopher
Brooke on which much of the work
of Basso & Brooke is based, such as
the design to the right, included in
the Fall/Winter 2007–2008 collection
presented at London Fashion Week.

Photography by Fernanda Calfat

- What inspires you?

We inspire each other. Technology is extremely inspirational for us. We like our work to have an eye on the past but an even closer eye on the future. We always look outside of fashion for inspiration; it is in our nature. We are inspired by brilliant design in whatever form it may take—fine arts, science and social behavior are our current interests.

- What is your dream as a designer?

There are many: to develop a new aesthetic, to be inspiring, to be remembered for bringing something new to fashion, to be consumed.

- What has been the most important achievement of your career?

Winning the first Fashion Fringe and having a garment from our first full collection (Fall/Winter 2005–2006) in the permanent collection of New York's Metropolitan Museum of Art.

- How important are trends?

We look to trends to gauge the relevance of silhouettes and general mood, but we take what we need. We are not a trend-led design house.

- Fashion has always reflected a certain era. What does fashion reflect in the twenty-first century?

The power of the customer. They are extremely important in contemporary fashion. Now they dictate what they want and how they want it. It's time for the new establishment. People want to consume "new." The industry has followed it and reviewed the concept of mass production. For example, in one single collection, we can handle over 100 prints using digital printing, naturally making each piece more exclusive, which would have been financially impractical in the past. Although we don't necessarily agree with it, celebrity endorsement has also certainly become an important PR tool for established fashion houses, as well as young designers.

- What book would you recommend to every fashion designer?

The Art of Manipulating Fabric by Colette Wolff.

Basso & Brooke
76 Bushey Hill Road
London SE5 8QJ
United Kingdom
www.bassoandbrooke.com

Sketch courtesy of Basso & Brooke

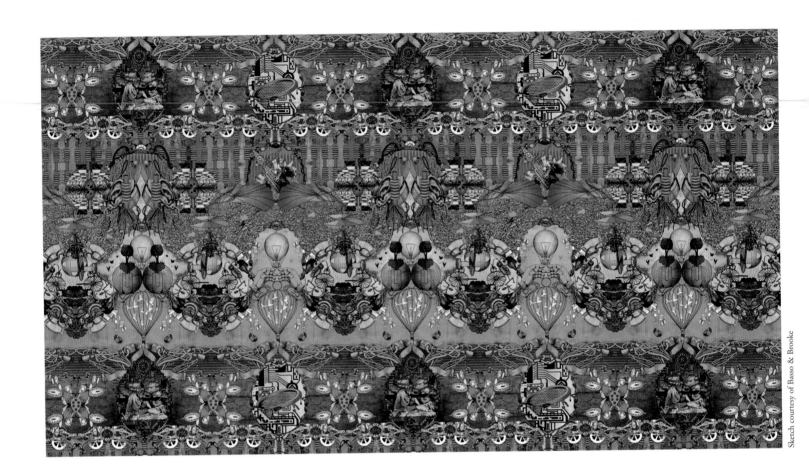

Sketch courtesy of Basso & Brooke

Image from the Spring/Summer
2007 collection in which the Roaring
20s serve as a point of departure.
Unmistakable nods to French designer
Paul Poiret are coupled with an almost
wild exuberance characteristic of the
fashion house.

Photography by Fernanda Calfat

Sketch courtesy of Basso & Brooke

Photography by Fernanda Calfat

With a palette of pastel tones and an aesthetic geometry that recalls the 80s, designers Brooke and Basso presented their Spring/Summer 2008 collection, from which this image is taken.

© Damien Blottiere

Bernhard Willhelm

Once in a while, the fashion universe gets shaken up by designers who defy conventional tastes with collections that are as unique and full of color as they are brazen. Such is the case of Bernhard Willhelm, whose work, the fruit of this creative anarchy, is impossible to classify. It is no surprise, then, that he attracts other artists such as Björk, who has done something similar with music. The fusion of the avant-garde itself, blazing trails that only it dares to follow.

Bernhard studied fashion design at the University of Antwerp. He then went on to work as an assistant for designers such as Walter Van Beirendonck, Alexander McQueen, Vivienne Westwood and Dirk Bikkembergs.

Since the presentation of his first collection, Bernhard has continued to follow a path on the frontier of the usual. Recycling, vintage, colorful garments, the revision of Bavarian folklore bathed in acid culture, knits, and combinations brimming with humor. Designs soaked with an authenticity that makes a dissection of his influences and frigid analysis of his work utterly impossible. Aesthetics passed through a centrifuge in the generation of a unique product: indivisible.

All of this makes Bernhard a source of inspiration for artists of diverse disciplines, as well as an icon of brazenness and creative stimulation. An artist who expresses himself by assembling in his collections the deconstructed fragments of fashion in order to create that which is unique. A designer who unwittingly creates trends and stimulates minds with his humor, irreverence, and genius.

© Claus Geis

Photography by Carmen Freudenthal/Ellen Verhagen

Women's collection from the
Spring/Summer 2007 season in which
Willhelm explores the concept of
street, fun and chic, demonstrating his
preference for expressive colors without
ever forgetting his Bavarian roots.

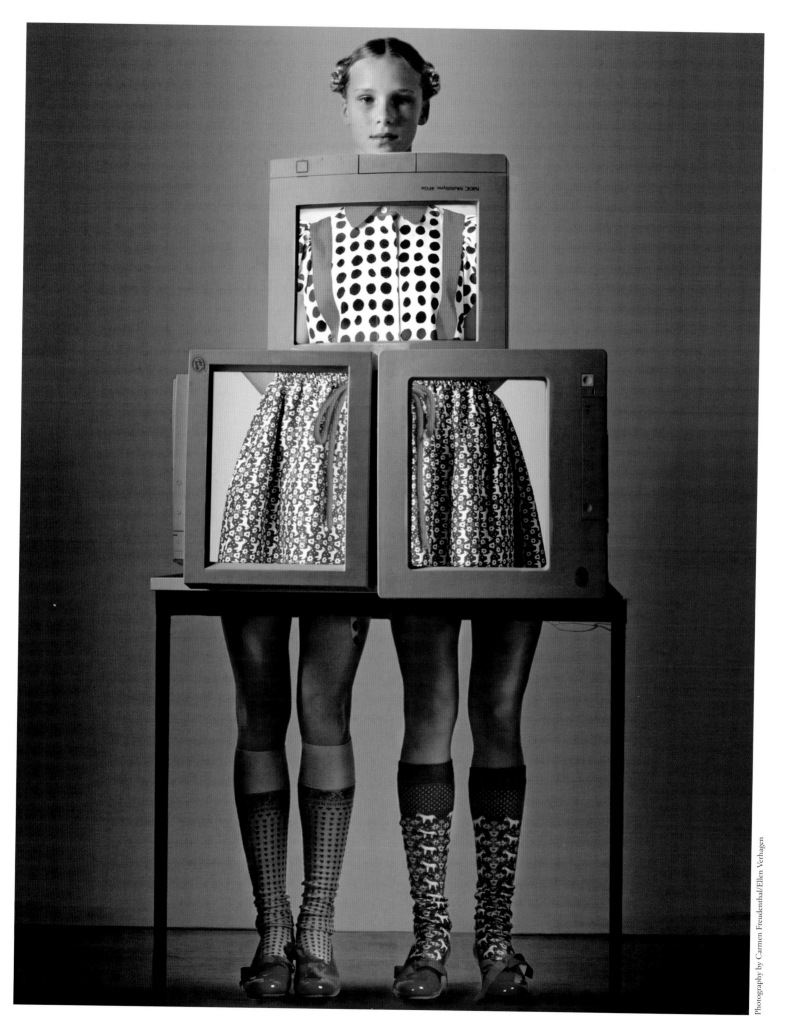

Bernhard Willhelm

Photography by Carmen Freudenthal/Ellen Verhagen

- What inspires you?

What I love and inspires me most: birds flying towards us and then flying away again; the moments between moments, when you're happy; coffee with two guests and a dog; streets made of golden sunlight; meat and dumplings at home; the high of sex; a lot of money when we earn it—not later, when we spend it; art at the moment it's created; something too expensive that we can afford; a certain smile; elephant showers; death, as long as we're not dying.

- What is your dream as a designer?

To keep my traveling ticket in order to remember where to get out.

- What has been the most important achievement of your career?

To buy my own presents.

- How important are trends?

Sometimes it is enough to put your ring on the other finger or your wristwatch on the other hand.

- Fashion has always reflected a certain era. What does fashion reflect in the twenty-first century?

Cheap crap made in the Far East by people with slavery-like work conditions.

- What book would you recommend to every fashion designer?

A Filofax, Google, YouTube, AstrologyZone.com.

Bernhard Willhelm

5 bis, rue Martel

75010 Paris

France

bernhard.willhelm@wanadoo.fr

103
Bernhard Willhelm

© Maria Ziegelbock

© Maria Ziegelbock

Images from his Spring/Summer 2008
men's collection, inspired by North
American wrestlers and in which
French porn star François Sagat
collaborated as a model.

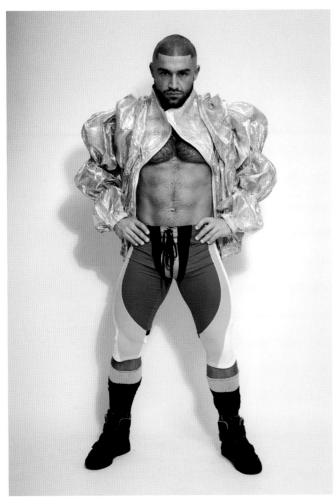

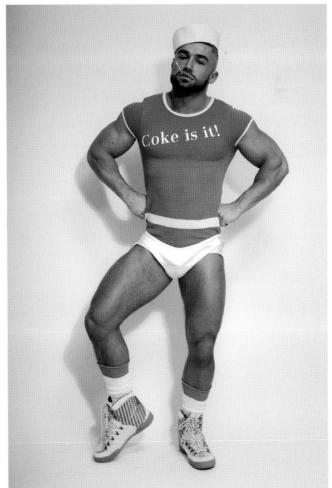

© Maria Ziegelbock

Photography by Almond Chu

Blanc de Chine

Fashion is a social phenomenon intrinsically joined to the nervous excitement of change, of the ephemeral. It is by no means a temporary condition, but rather it is an attitude. The search for the intangible brought to fruition in coats, scarves and accessories that change with each season and define an irreverent and dizzying universe.

Each year, hundreds of designs, thousands of paths to go down, a millions avenues that open up and fork off into others. One of these bypasses winds down to an unusual place: Blanc de Chine. By uniting tradition with modernity, the ephemeral with the durable, Blanc de Chine seeks to halt the accelerated rhythm of fashion, assembling the scattered space-time fragments of post-modernity in garments that are placid and serene, creations which evoke the past and usher in tranquility, ones that generate a slow tempo and a space of silence. To this end, the spirit and aesthetic of one of the eternal icons of spirituality is summoned forth: ancient China.

The *qipao, dudou* and *zhongshan* are some of the traditional Chinese garments elegantly adapted to Western ways—not only to Western tastes, but to its particular rhythms and lifestyle. All of the clothes of Blanc de Chine are exquisitely designed and tailored employing ancient traditional methods and unique fabrics that accompany us nicely in our day-to-day lives, as well as on special occasions.

A reinterpretation of Chinese classics. A significant luxury item that resists ostentation as well as the fleetingness which, year after year, invades the showcase windows of cities everywhere. A balm for modern life.

Sketch courtesy of Blanc de Chine

Photography by Almond Chu

The "Dao" collection brings us closer to tradition through the revision of an ancient lingerie garment, the *dudou*: pure, basic forms that play with the dimensionality of the fabric and salvage simplicity for our lives.

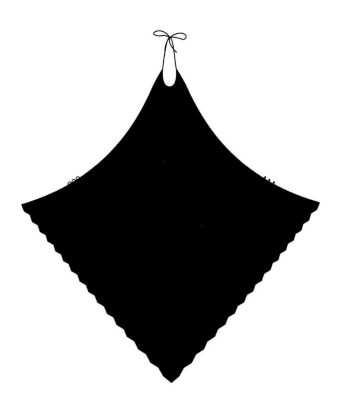

Leather silk pleated du dou dress

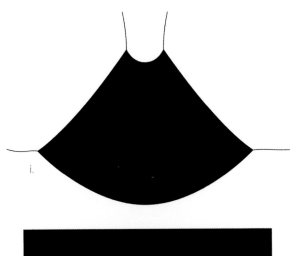

i.

ii.

i. Classic leather silk du dou
ii. Leather silk long rectangular wrap skirt

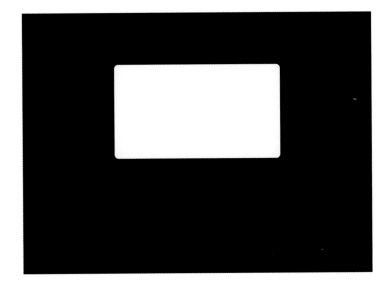

i. Reversible silk rectangular vest, can be doubled as a saddle bag.
Black drawstring chiffon pants

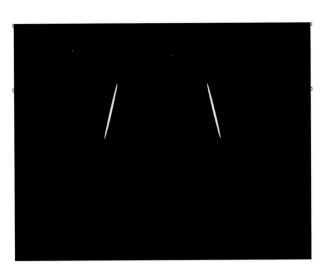

Leather silk blanket coat

Technical drawings courtesy of Blanc de Chine

- What inspires you?

Nowadays, the word "Chinese" generally connotes cheapness and mediocrity. However, as recently as the eighteenth century and before, the West looked to the East for quality and excellence. We share this aspiration and hope to pioneer the renaissance of Chinese art and culture.

- What is your dream as a designer?

My dream is to see Blanc de Chine in prominent corners of all major cities across the world and to stand out among other leading luxury brands.

- What has been the most important achievement of your career?

I have done a total of three constructional projects in Manhattan: development of a thirty-three storey residential condominium (the Octavia at 47th Street), a four storey mixed-use building at East 46th Street and the Blanc de Chine Flagship store at 673 5th Avenue. Two of my three projects have been recognized with important awards: the Progressive Architecture Award (the Octavia, 1983) and Contract Magazine's Best Retail Interior Design Award (Blanc de Chine, 2006).

So, my interests go beyond fashion design to architectural design and interior design, even furniture design.

As for fashion design, Blanc de Chine is gathering international recognition as the first luxury brand from China.

- How important are trends?

Blanc de Chine is not too concerned with trends, since most of our pieces are designed to be timeless. Ignoring trends enables us to break the time barrier, cruise from the past to the unbounded future and come back with something both functional and beautiful for the present.

- Fashion has always reflected a certain era. What does fashion reflect in the twenty-first century?

Globalization will accelerate convergence of multiple cultures from all corners of the world. Fashion will no longer be monopolized by Western culture alone. The convergence of cultures creates options for alternative lifestyles. Blanc de Chine is more than clothing design. Our ultimate goal is to come up with a complete range of lifestyle products consistent with the Blanc de Chine spirit.

- What book would you recommend to every fashion designer?

I don't think it is appropriate to recommend any particular book to other designers. I suggest we read as much as possible. The more widely read, the better a designer's ability to come up with stronger concepts and designs. Zen reading has freed me from fixation and enabled me to shuttle between the realms of imagination and reality.

Blanc de Chine
673 5th Avenue
New York, NY 10022
United States
www.blancdechine.com

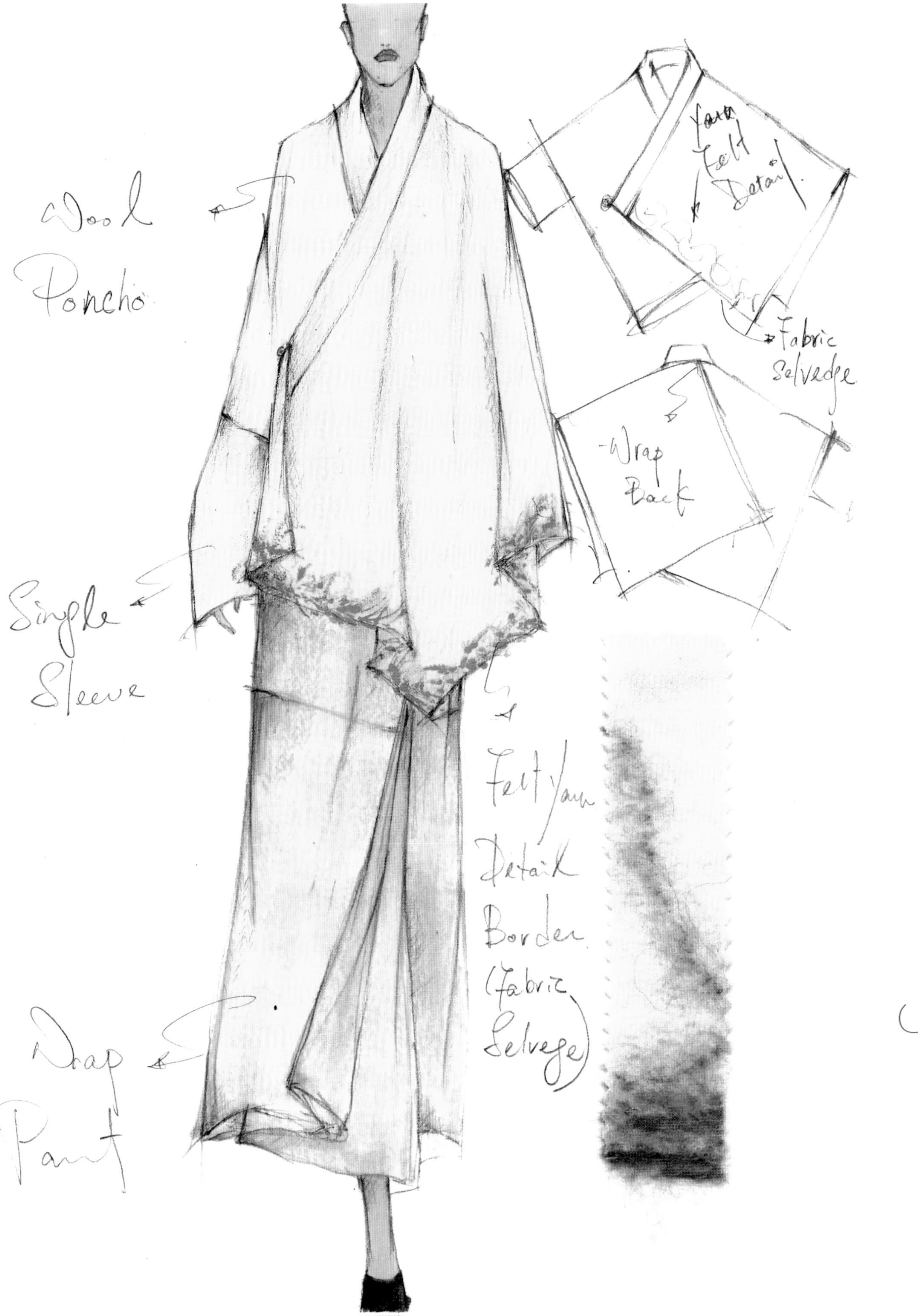

Wool Poncho

Single Sleeve

Drap Pant

Yarn Felt Detail

Fabric Selvedge

Wrap Back

Felt Yarn Detail Border (Fabric Selvege)

Sketch courtesy of Blanc de Chine

Silk Chiffon
Twisted Top

Silk
GGT
Wide Pant

C
F

C
B

Twist
To
Front

Sketch courtesy of Blanc de Chine

One of the principal successes of Kin Yeung, founder and designer of Blanc de Chine, has been his acumen for selecting the best of China's cultural richness and applying it to fashion, as these sketches make undoubtedly clear.

2 Squares Top

In Crinkle Silk

Double Candle Button

See through
Silk Chiffon
Guset

Crinkle Silk Flare Pant

Sketch courtesy of Blanc de Chine

Photography by Andreas Schlegel

Bless

Bless is a concave mirror within the world of fashion, a way of viewing reality with ingenuity and creativity that transcends the established frontiers demarcating design, art and recycling. For this reason, there are few images of Germans Desiree Heiss and Ines Kaag. They are the ones who are watching, not the ones being watched, the ones who decide to explore the convolutions of the quotidian in order to reinvent the most mundane objects and garments with humor and lucidity, an original and comic mix of disparate genres that results in the creation of unique and impossible objects. Gorgeous.

Bless's conception of reality does not recognize the conventional limits of fashion, design and life. Nonexistent is the fundamental boundary between what is "distinctive" and what is "ordinary." All merges in a disturbing, studied, and astute way, giving rise to compositions charged with suggestiveness and humor that undermine the established order through unconventional aesthetics.

Its breathtaking cable jewels, the vacuum cleaner chair, the sitting wall as an urban project, the comfortable yet functional bag towel and the winter crochet glasses are among Bless's most outstanding accessories and objects. A hybridization that bursts onto the fashion design scene with espadrille slippers, scarves made from pants and sweaters, and the acknowledged influence of Martin Margiela and Helmut Lang in recycled and deconstructed garments. Two female artists with an independent style struggling against mass individuality. An intellectual distancing regarding an aesthetic full of irony and wit. A conceptual way of understanding reality replete with humor. Undiluted visual poetry.

Photography courtesy of Bless

Photography courtesy of Bless

Photography courtesy of Bless

If anything characterizes Desiree
Heiss and Ines Kaag, founders of the
Bless label, it is their great sense of
humor and capacity for breaking with
convention, as this wig-shirt makes
undoubtedly clear.

- What inspires you?

Everyday life.

- What is your dream as a designer?

For things we create to fulfill needs, make people happy and get used.

- What has been the most important achievement of your career?

To meet each other!

- How important are trends?

If a trend were motivating people to get something else to improve their lives and feel better, it would be as essential as a natural catastrophe could be to stop pollution in an over-saturated world.

- Fashion has always reflected a certain era. What does fashion reflect in the twenty-first century?

Better to ask in the next century. It's always easier to reflect over the past.

- What book would you recommend to every fashion designer?

A multilingual dictionary.

Bless
14, rue Portefoin
75003 Paris
France
www.bless-service.de

Photography courtesy of Bless

Photography by Andreas Schlegel

Photography by Andreas Schlegel

In this Fall/Winter 2007–2008
collection entitled "Ohyescoolgreat,"
Bless offers us diverse garments with
a common denominator: they are
conceived for all kinds of people,
without set patterns. Different clothes
for different people.

Photographies courtesy of Bless

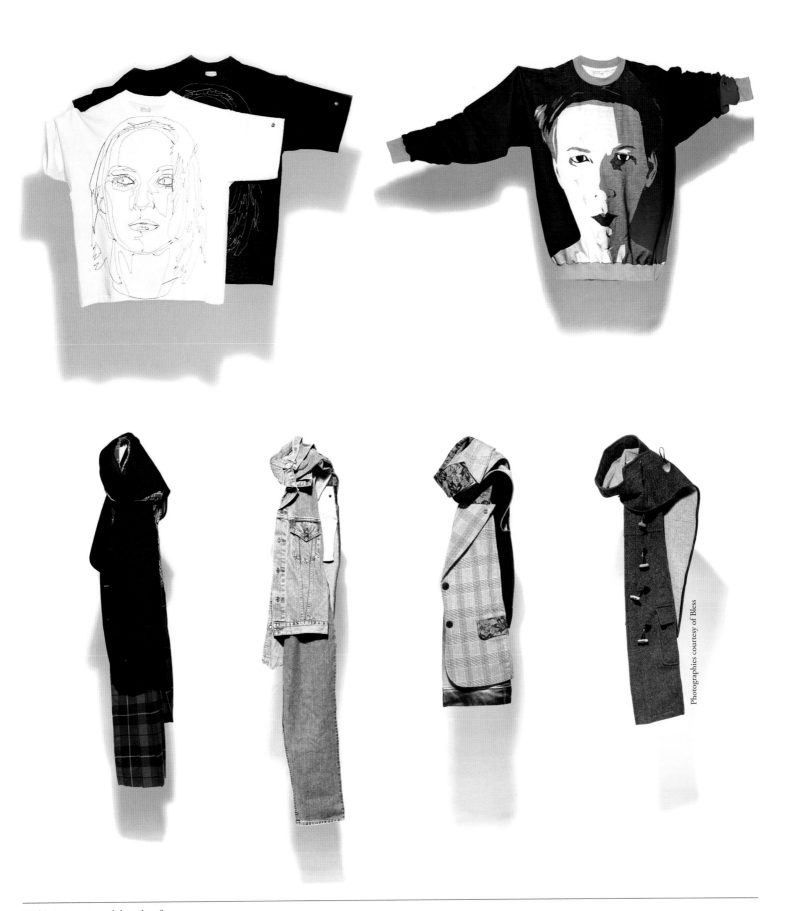

Photographies courtesy of Bless

Within in its unique philosophy of fashion, Bless proposes with its 1999 "Merchandising" collection a series of unisize, unisex and uniage creations as a way of escaping the stereotypes that prevail on fashion runways.

Sketch courtesy of Bora Aksu

Bora Aksu

The clothing of Bora Aksu is conceived for running through the country, for traveling, so that the pleats, capes and bows that make up his ensembles flutter in the wind. The noble materials, the hats and the quality wools are suggestive of a certain ancient nomadic spirit, one halfway between the cosmopolitan London catwalk and the influence of Turkey, the designer's native country. A graduate of London's Central Saint Martins College, Boro quickly captured the attention of the specialized press, as well as designers as prestigious as Domenico Dolce and Stefano Gabbana. He received the Top Shop New Generation Prize on two occasions in 2004 for his Spring/Summer and Fall/Winter collections and again in 2005 for his Spring/Summer collection. From there, he went on to become a regular at London Fashion Week. His collaborations beyond the world of fashion have been diverse. They include fashioning the wardrobe of Tori Amos, a collection of sports shoes for Converse and the designs for the performance given by contemporary dance company The Cathy Marston Project at the Royal Opera House in London.

The fabrics employed by Bora are characterized by natural tones—a brown, ochre and carmine palette in winter and a clear and luminous one in summer—that suffuse the pleats of tunics and the ribbons that provide relief and tie loose, vaporous dresses. These are garments that hint at change, at movement. Indeed, the collaboration between this designer and a contemporary dance group is no coincidence. In the face of rigidity and corseting, features commonly associated with elegance, Bora proposes free movement and fluidity, embracing the mutability of life with an unusual and meticulous elegance. In short, these are sensible garments in step with the rhythm of life.

Photography courtesy of Bora Aksu

Bora Aksu

Sketch courtesy of Bora Aksu

Photographies by Ian Giller

Images from the Fall/Winter 2007–2008
collection. On the project, Bora Aksu
worked with Artisan Armours, which
has participated in films such as *Troy*,
Alexander the Great and *King Arthur*. From
this collaboration emerged some of the
designer's most spectacular pieces to date.

- What inspires you?

Objects from everyday life inspire me. I always start out with something very personal, such as experiences, thoughts. The collection always relates to my personal and spiritual journey. To me, creativity is very sensitive, and collaborating with people from different art fields is very inspiring. My recent collaboration with the Artisan Armours group was also a true inspiration to me, being in their environment and seeing their passion for their work.

- What is your dream as a designer?

To me, creativity is a very sensitive and personal way of expressing yourself. It's almost your unique language to communicate with the world without using actual words. Therefore, my dream would be to create a whole wardrobe for a periodic-futuristic movie.

- What has been the most important achievement of your career?

I guess it has been being able to create, which I love to do, and still earn my living by it. Designing is something that you absolutely love and cannot do without. It's a passion, but it doesn't feel like it's taking too much time because it's your hobby more than it's a job.

- How important are trends?

I believe fashion is more of a way of expressing someone's individuality rather than just a simple way of covering the body parts. It is a unique language that has a visual voice. As individualism becomes the new trend, people are searching for uniqueness. I am a designer who really does not follow trends.

- Fashion has always reflected a certain era. What does fashion reflect in the twenty-first century?

Fashion and women's approach to it has changed so dramatically over the last decades. Women today are much more aware of who they are and what they want to achieve in their lives. I don't really believe that fashion will ever become a statement like it was in the 50s or 60s. The world is changing so quickly, and women are more aware of what they like and who they are. I do not like to tell my clients how they should dress. My designs or the way I put them together in a fashion show is just a suggestion from the designer. It's completely up to the person how she would like to wear that garment. I love the way they add their personalities to a garment and make it alive.

- What book would you recommend to every fashion designer?

The Bible.

Bora Aksu
130 Milligan Street
London E14 8AS
United Kingdom
www.boraaksu.com

Sketch courtesy of Bora Aksu

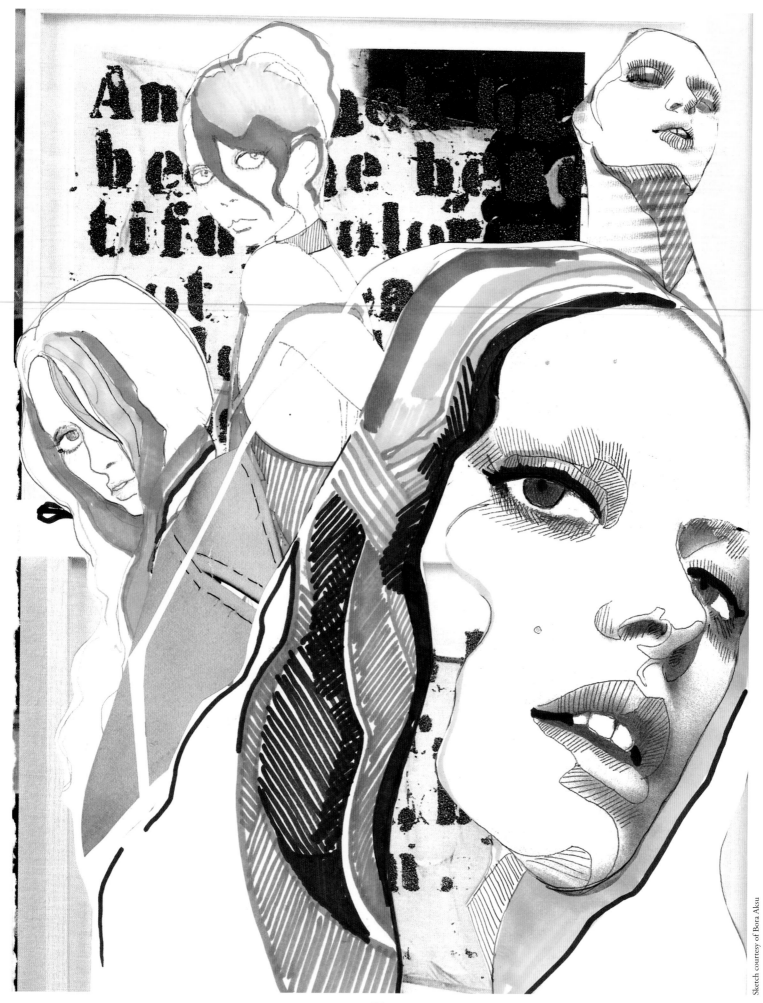

Sketch courtesy of Bora Aksu

Sketch courtesy of Bora Aksu

Evidence of Bora Aksu's artistic talent,
these illustrations serve as the basis for
the designer's collections, noteworthy
for their movement, lightness and
search for simplicity within glamour
and sophistication.

Cathy Pill

© Gregory Derkenne

Cathy Pill

The darling designer of French fashion was born in Belgium, where she studied at the Superior School of Fine Arts, quickly evolving from a young promise into an award-winning designer. On her bright trajectory to stardom, she has worked for such big names as A.F. Vandevorst, Vivienne Westwood, and Rochas. Her collection, Blink, was exhibited at the Louvre's Museum of Decorative Arts; and after very few collections, her label can be found in Australia, Austria, Japan, Belgium, Canada, France, Hong Kong, Kuwait, Spain, and Saudi Arabia.

To what is owed so much success in so little time? Cathy Pill creates beautiful, meticulous clothing. Vaporous dresses with an exquisite finish, perfect patterns, and surprising prints. With modernist echoes, her garments acknowledge this style without being shrill about it. Her studied, polished simplicity transforms a woman into a gorgeous effigy, salvaging the mysterious quality of another time through a modern, essentialist design.

This is because every last detail on a Cathy Pill creation abounds with good taste and delicacy. Hers is an aesthetic universe which unostentatiously recreates a feminine woman with silk dresses, insinuating shadows, and draped silhouettes. Cathy has demonstrated her skill for rehabilitating a kind of harmonious sophistication that gives rise to beauty naturally, free of artifice and pretense, through her more than proven mastery of volumes.All of this makes her one of the most promising designers of a generation trained by such brilliant and renowned figures as Vandevorst and the great Westwood. A priceless gem of the latest generation.

© Gregory Derkenne

134
Cathy Pill

© Gregory Derkenne

© Gregory Derkenne

Carving out a niche for oneself on the demanding Paris runway is no easy task, but Cathy Pill has done precisely this, thanks to the strength of her personality and the exquisite care she takes with her ethereal cuts and exceptional prints.

- What inspires you?

I'm greatly inspired by structures and architecture. I'm working with my eyes and fingers. I'm not a storyteller in my collections; I'm more expressing feelings or ideas. The art nouveau period is a great inspiration for me, especially the idea that every detail has a sense of being and is a part of a global structure.

- What is your dream as a designer?

Working further on my designs, expanding the collections with assorted accessories, continuing to experience other fields in the art and exploring the world a lot better.

- What has been the most important achievement of your career?

To see women wearing my clothes with pleasure.

- How important are trends?

Not as important as having your own style. People are finally searching for a real personality. Trends are changing; a personal style is not.

- Fashion has always reflected a certain era. What does fashion reflect in the twenty-first century?

The world has become very small in the twenty-first century. People are constantly curious, searching for new volumes, new techniques, new technology, always wanting to go further, forever.

- What book would you recommend to every fashion designer?

Vionnet by Jacqueline Demornex (Éditions du Regard).

Cathy Pill
7, rue d'Alost
1000 Brussels
Belgium
www.cathypill.com

Cathy Pill

© Raf Thienpont

© Raf Thienpont

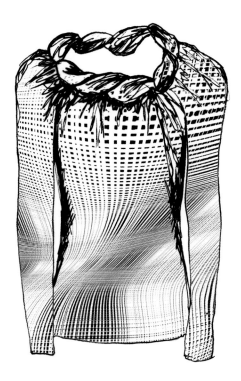
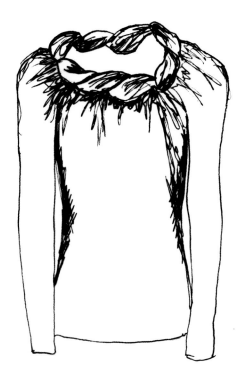
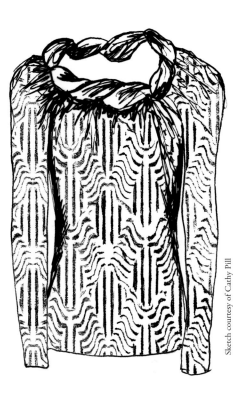

Sketch courtesy of Cathy Pill

Image from the Spring/Summer 2008
"Untouched" collection, characterized
by geometric motifs in black and
white, embodied in creations replete
with strength, delicacy and dynamism.

Claudia Rosa Lukas

Michael Dürr/model: Raoni (Flair Vienna)

Claudia Rosa Lukas

Helmut Lang's outstanding student, Claudia Rosa Lukas, a young Austrian who in the course of her short career has demonstrated her command of the lessons learned from Helmut and Vivienne Westwood, successfully integrating the best teachings of the previous generation into her own artistic vision. All of this makes Claudia the visible sign of evolution in fashion design, the natural continuation of a phase well digested, with sufficient strength to continue illuminating and inspiring designers to come.

Claudia was born in Austria and studied at the Universities of Vienna and Berlin. She soon made a name for herself, obtaining the Ministry of Science and Transportation Prize and the Austrian Fashion Award for contemporary design.

The work of Claudia Rosa is not rupturing, but harmonious. Claudia confidently incorporates details into her creations that at another time were considered revolutionary, lessons learned by someone who has mastered her trade. Without fuss or sharp turns. With harmony, care and elegance. Allowing details to emerge gracefully, thus endowing garments with a meticulous feminine touch.

To this end, this Austrian designer creates exquisite designs that result in tidy, refined garments. This gives rise to a meticulous sobriety with flat colors and stylized figures that provide sophistication and femininity to women who do not require a grand display to attract attention. A studied, natural, and beautiful simplicity that unites the radical aspect of the aesthetic legacy of big names in fashion history with the well-balanced freedom of a highly talented young designer.

Photography by Nile M.

Claudia Rosa Lukas

Michael Dürr/model: Anna (Tempo Models)

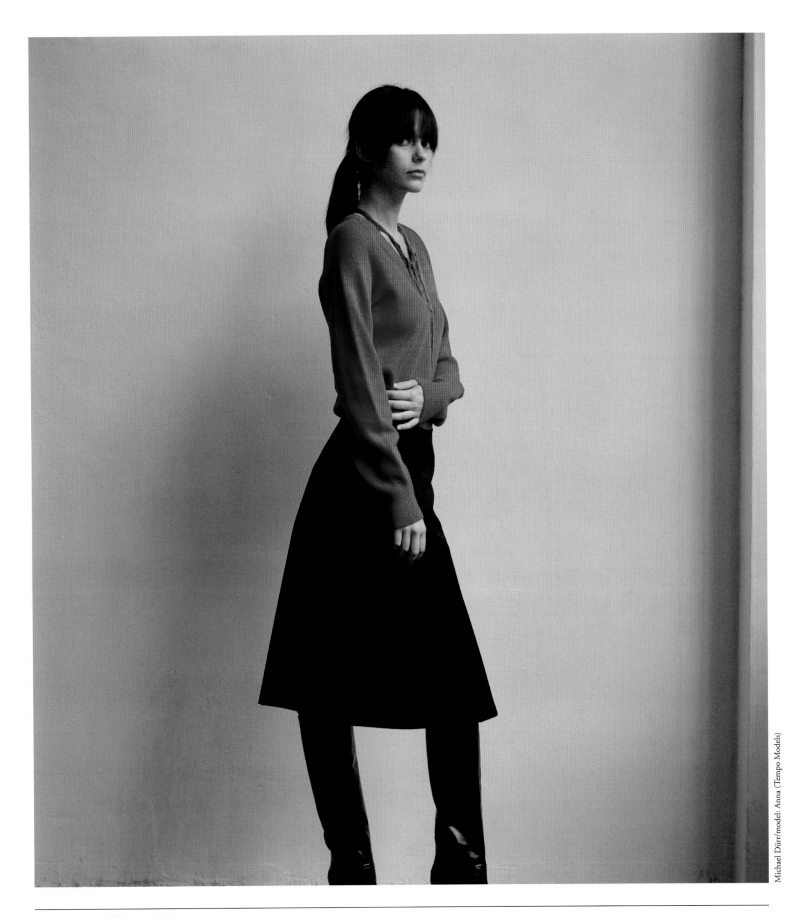

Michael Dürr/model: Anna (Tempo Models)

Images from the Fall/Winter 2006–
2007 season in which the Austrian
designer presents a collection in three
colors—white, black and bright
flaming red—that awakens the senses
opposite the discretion of other tones.

- What inspires you?

It always depends on everything that's going on. Influences are everywhere, mainly people around me and their way of thinking, living and acting.

- What is your dream as a designer?

Imagine if design could change the world. Apparently, this will forever remain a dream.

- What has been the most important achievement of your career?

Every finished collection.

- How important are trends?

I am a very attentive trend-watcher. Above all, tendencies in the fields of science, politics, economics and entertainment have an increasingly strong influence on fashion.

- Fashion has always reflected a certain era. What does fashion reflect in the twenty-first century?

Anything goes. People love changes and new materials. The best advertising strategies will show us the way where it will go.

- What book would you recommend to every fashion designer?

Every designer should be aware of the past. I would recommend exploring different costume histories and books about black-and-white portrait photography.

Claudia Rosa Lukas

Pramergasse 6-1-22

1090 Vienna

Austria

www.lukas-by.com

Michael Dürr/model: Anna (Tempo Models)

145
Claudia Rosa Lukas

Michael Dürr/model: Lukas (Tempo Models)/jewelry by Sonja Bischur in Lukas in black shirt

Within her simple, sharp lines, Claudia
Rosa Lukas includes this series of
shirts in her Fall/Winter 2006–2007
collection that articulates the lines of
a square in an intriguing and playful
way.

Claudia Rosa Lukas

Michael Dürr/model: Hanna Putz

Claudia Rosa Lukas

Sketch by Claudia Rosa Lukas

Sketches in which the designer,
through a combination of
photography, illustration and
graphic design, defines what her next
collections will be and puts forward
that sophisticated sobriety of hers to
which we have become accustomed.

Sketch by Claudia Rosa Lukas

Photography by Michael Dürr/model: Raoni (Flair Vienna)

Claudia Rosa Lukas

Photography by Michael Dürr/model: Raoni (Flair Vienna)

Complex details within a studied
simplicity. White, ivory and black
tones, pure cuts and high quality
materials are the fundamental
features of this Spring/Summer 2006
collection.

Photography by Tim Griffiths

Clements Ribeiro

When two talented designers enjoy what they're doing, there's something that cannot be easily remedied: designs burst with color, prints invade dresses and blouses, and traditional elegance becomes somewhat irreverent, as if a torrent of happiness had flooded the work and displaced a certain rigidity and formality with new and unusual creations.

This is the case of Brazilian designer Inácio Ribeiro and British designer Suzanne Clements. Their joyful alliance radiates ingenuity and mastery in each and every one of their creations. So it's no surprise, then, that the two designers have become a reference for innovation within British fashion. They met at Central Saint Martins and soon thereafter founded Clements Ribeiro, making a name for themselves with an eclectic, feminine and very unconventional first collection. Since then, their groundbreaking style has brought them numerous awards for its graceful fusion of elegance, quality and diversity. At its core is an exquisite combination of attention to cut and finish and a sharp sensibility for uniting fabrics and textures. Desirous of making this unique identity its own, from 2000 until 2007, legendary brand Cacharel ceded creative control of its collections to Clements Ribeiro. Since then, the designers have dedicated their energies exclusively to their own label.

Clements Ribeiro is a special coalition, truly unique. It would have been easy to find a niche in the fashion world through tremendous display, excessive ornamentation and disparate combinations, yet Clements Ribeiro elected a different path. Still, the special feature of these two designers' work does lie in a kind of studied imbalance, or rather, a balanced oscillation between bohemianism and elegance.

Photography by Tim Griffiths

To the right, image from backstage
belonging to the eclectic and nostalgic
Fall/Winter 2005–2006 collection.
Above, more backstage images from
the Spring/Summer 2005 collection,
with a marked 50s influence.

Photography by Tim Griffiths

Photography by Tim Griffiths

- What inspires you?

We are passionate about the visual arts, particularly paintings and drawings. We are museum rats and art bookworms. We are also constantly traveling. And we don't mean only business trips, but mostly road trips and adventure trips, and along the way we have collected many objects and souvenirs. Over the years we have found ourselves using these things as research objects. Fashion itself has always been a major energizer, past and present.

- What is your dream as a designer?

To make great clothes that reflect uniqueness and craftsmanship, as well as relevance to our customer and our times.

- What has been the most important achievement of your career?

To have maintained our integrity and our relationship throughout all the inevitable ups and downs of a successful fashion career.

- How important are trends?

They facilitate the spread of certain ideas that seem to capture a moment. They are to "happen" as opposed to being imposed or to being followed. The creative impulse in its most individual expression is our true pleasure.

- Fashion has always reflected a certain era. What does fashion reflect in the twenty-first century?

So far, we believe fashion this century has shown a very dynamic struggle between huge brand corporations and the creative resistance by independent houses. All seems to be on the brink of change, and as we all chase to capture that essence, fashion becomes very plural and of very high standards both in creativity and craft. Changing periods are always very exciting and therefore very creative, in both design and strategy.

- What book would you recommend to every fashion designer?

Tom Wolfe's *The Bonfire of the Vanities* is as good as any an introduction to all the perils of trading on people's vanities and their social mores.

Clements Ribeiro
claire@clementsribeiro.com

Photography by Tim Griffiths

157

Clements Ribeiro

© Stefano Guindani/Costume National Archives

Costume National

Costume National is the fruit of the influence of Japan on Italy, of the Japanese bath of purification, of the bustle of the Italian street.

Behind Costume National is Ennio Capasa, a graduate of Milan's Accademia di Belle Arti di Brera, who, after completing his studies, was offered the unparalleled opportunity of traveling to Japan to work with Yohji Yamamoto, with whom he collaborated for three years.

Returning to Italy, he founded the brand Costume National along with his brother Carlo, who had previously worked as an advisor to Dawn Melo at Gucci. Ennio borrowed the name from a French book of uniforms given to him by Carlo.

Their first collection appeared in Italy in the mid-80s, clearly not the ideal moment for the blend of rounded femininity and Japanese refinement Ennio had absorbed so well in Japan and was now proposing: a woman free of angles and straight lines, one with more realistic and attractive contours who defied the aesthetic canons of the day. This led to Ennio's decision to step out onto the international stage and make a name for himself. In 1983, he presented a line of shoes, followed by leather accessories, bags and lingerie in 2000, his first line of perfume in 2002 and his first eyewear collection in 2003.

Costume National represents the combination of experience and know-how with which Ennio develops his talent, embodied in genuine, recognizable work that stands out among the whirlpool of images and visual identities of contemporary society.

© Settimio Benedusi

On the first page, a design from the Fall/
Winter 2007–2008 collection in which
Capasa unites different worlds—uniforms
and dresses—and which represents only the
beginning of Costume National. On these
pages, images from the Spring/Summer
2007 collection.

© Sofia Sánchez & Mauro Mongiello (Katy Barker Agency)/model: Julia Dunstall

- What inspires you?

An inexhaustible source of inspiration is the Italian cinema of the 60s and the 70s. The aesthetics were absolutely perfect. And, of course, rock and roll and punk music. And modern art in general.

- What is your dream as a designer?

I would love not being forced by deadlines, but that is a utopian dream, regardless of the business you are in. I would be happy if I could believe in the next generation, but they seem to have no dreams, no interest any more. Today, Italian fashion is blocked. There are no healthy exchanges in fashion houses. I really hope young, creative people will be more daring and audacious.

- What has been the most important achievement of your career?

Being able to remain independent even when fashion was the center of big groups' business and financial strategies. It allows me to go on being creative with no limitations or pressure.

- How important are trends?

Trends are always important, but fashion has become more versatile. Nowadays, everybody is free to express their own personality through the way they dress. Being trendy is not what counts the most anymore; it is much more important to be true to your own style.

- Fashion has always reflected a certain era. What does fashion reflect in the twenty-first century?

Today's fashion points towards the respect of the body. The silhouettes are closer to the body, leaner, gentler in a way. Soft curves are allowed, there is more room for genuine femininity. Conceptual fashion is over, momentum is not on the brand any more but on the individual. The new luxury means precious natural materials; fabrics that allow the body to move, cuts and shapes that combines freedom and sophistication. That's really what my work has been about since the very beginning.

- What book would you recommend to every fashion designer?

The Picture of Dorian Gray.

Costume National
Via Mario Fusetti, 12
20143 Milan
Italy
www.costumenational.com

© Sofía Sánchez & Mauro Mongiello (Katy Barker Agency)/model: Julia Dunstall

© Sofia Sánchez & Mauro Mongiello (Kary Barker Agency)/model: Mathias Lauridsen

To the left, Fall/Winter 2008–2009
collection. To the right, the Spring/
Summer 2007 collection. Light
garments that cloak the wearer in a
second skin, with silver tones and
a metallic shine that simulate the
reflection of seawater.

© Sofia Sánchez & Mauro Mongiello (Kary Barker Agency)/model: Jakob Hedberg

Photography by Rudy Archuleta

Craig Robinson

If Craig Robinson had lived in the New York of the 20s, he would have been the tailor of gangsters and mafiosos. The darling designer of suits worn to speakeasies in the Era of Prohibition. The whim of a mob boss with taste. The principal architect of the distinguished and arrogant style of a romantic time.

For this reason, today, in the absence of other icons of raffish elegance, Craig dresses the bad boys of downtown New York, groups like Interpol, the New York Dolls and Secret Machines, among others, are some of his most fervent followers. All of them visit his workshop on 5th Avenue, where respect and reverence for the creative process of the tailor is palpable, where clients are treated with the same courtesy and affection with which Craig designs, cuts and sews their suits, suits that combine elegant tailoring with a current touch, resulting in a unique and singular garment customized to the personality of its owner.

Since he was young, this New Mexico–born designer exhibited a passion for dress garments and a skill for coming up with cowboy outfits for his friends. It is likely that this experience helped him realize that the same suit takes on a different character depending on who is wearing it and that only through customized work is it possible to obtain the appropriate look for an individual.

For this reason, on his webpage Craig is seen creating, drawing, sewing with his old machine in a dark, clandestine atmosphere, to the rhythm of rock and roll, making the creative process a delight—all a luxury in these times of stylism and pret-a-porter, a creation for those who know how to appreciate the mastery that goes into a unique suit.

Photography by Rudy Archuleta

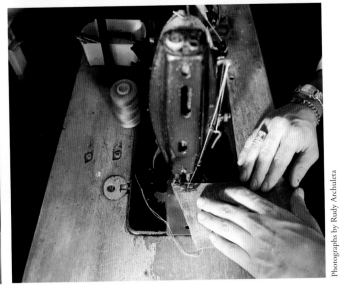

Photographs by Rudy Archuleta

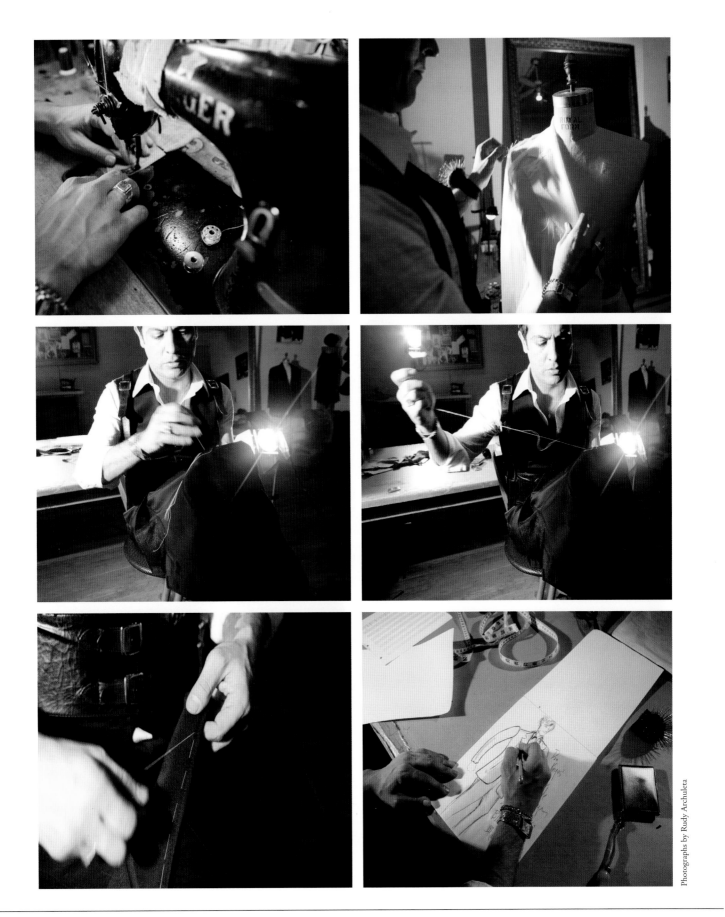

Images of the designer in his New York
studio where he invests each of his
garments with the spirit of traditional
tailoring while simultaneously
remaining innovative, keeping pace
with modern times to the rhythm of
rock and roll.

Photographs by Rudy Archuleta

- What inspires you?

The greatest thing about being a fashion designer is using all the inspiration you take in and putting it into your garments. I am inspired by so many things and so many people: the faces of my great city, the characters that are my clients, the daily hardships that one encounters living in New York—its sounds, colors, filth, architecture and, most of all, its greatness, its overwhelming size and charm.

- What is your dream as a designer?

As a fashion designer, my dream has been met in many ways, mainly in how I found my true love in life at such a young age. As far as goals are concerned, I hope to branch out from our clientele here in New York and other parts of the country and move into motion pictures.

- What has been the most important achievement of your career?

My most important achievement as a designer thus far has been earning the respect of my peers for my knowledge of garment construction and the quality of the product we produce. Achieving a signature look has always been something I'm very proud of, as well. I've always been aware of this in my designs from the time I began to the stage I'm at now.

- How important are trends?

I have always said I hate trends, but that is really hypocritical of me. It is my duty as a designer to create and set trends. Without trends, there is no competition, and no competition means no fun, no money and, ultimately, no survival.

- Fashion has always reflected a certain era. What does fashion reflect in the twenty-first century?

Fashion in the twenty-first century has become saturated with designers who have turned into publicity marketing machines. In past decades, we made a look for a specific person, but now clothing has been made to revolve around the perfect bag or belt or shoe. To most people in the industry, fashion is advertising.

- What book would you recommend to every fashion designer?

It would be my favorite book of design, *The Genius of Charles James*, a very unique look inside one designer's mind and life and the difficulties and triumphs of his career. This book can educate you on what to do and what not to do in order to accomplish your goals as a designer. I consider this book to be a look back at what it truly means to be a fashion designer.

Craig Robinson
144 5th Avenue, 3rd floor
New York, NY 10011
United States
www.craigrobinsonnyc.com

Photography by Rudy Archuleta

Craig Robinson

Photographs by Rudy Archuleta

Photography by Rudy Archuleta

From left to right, various musicians
dressed by the designer: Jon Spencer
(The Jon Spencer Blues Explosion),
Paul Banks (Interpol), Sammy Yaffa
(New York Dolls), Nuutti Kataja
(Dead Combo). On the right, Sharin
Foo (The Raveonettes).

Deepak Perwani

Photography by Tapu Javeri

Deepak Perwani

Since the beginning of his career, Deepak Perwani has been one of the most distinguished designers in his native country of Pakistan. In 1994, at the age of just twenty, he launched his first collection, which also happened to be the first men's collection ever in Pakistan, where until then fashion had been an exclusively female domain. The collection was based on a reconstruction of the *sherwani*, a long, coatlike garment worn in South Asia, and it turned Deepak into the enfant terrible of Pakistani fashion.

Later he began designing for women, as well. Currently, he designs four lines a year for men and women, in addition to haute couture work in which he has proven himself a master of his trade.

His success is due, in part, to his determination to represent a new Pakistani spirit, with creations that, without sacrificing his roots, are in contact with twenty-first century reality. From his first collection on, his progress and recognition have been unstoppable, as evidenced by his winning the prestigious Lux Style Prize, awarded annually to the best designer in Pakistani fashion, on three separate occasions.

Currently, he has four stores in Pakistan and plans to open three more in Karachi, Peshawar, and Dubai, in addition to opening his own showroom in London.

This uncommon designer who, in his own words, creates in order to satisfy an artistic restlessness, constitutes one of the maximum exponents of Pakistani fashion.

Photography by Tapu Javeri

Sketches by the Pakistani designer.

Deepak Perwani

- What inspires you?

The world inspires me: architecture, artists, colors, shapes, the nape of a neck, the beggar girl on the street, a beautiful smile. Inspiration has no boundaries, and I don't limit myself.

- What is your dream as a designer?

To go where no one has gone before. For me, the ultimate dream would be to win an Academy Award given by designers to designers.

- What has been the most important achievement of your career?

To have constantly pushed the boundaries of Pakistani fashion, to have brought it into the twenty-first century.

- How important are trends?

Trends are very important. They define a certain bond in a global village, as every designer takes inspiration from them and then coughs out his or her version of those guidelines.

- Fashion has always reflected a certain era. What does fashion reflect in the twenty-first century?

Fashion in the twenty-first century is truly the melting pot of what has been done from the 20s through the 80s, rehashed, refurbished, regenerated. From Poiret to Paco Rabanne, from *Mad Max* to *Barbarella*, everything has been revised, chewed and presented with the more sophisticated look of the sexual twenty-first century.

- What book would you recommend to every fashion designer?

The Royal Costumes of India by Ritu Kumar.

Deepak Perwani
Shop 1, 16-C, Zamzama Commercial
Lane 4, D.H.A. Karachi
Pakistan
www.deepakperwani.com

Deepak Perwani

Photography by Tapu Javeri

Fusing East and West, Deepak Perwani
attempts to establish the new foundations of Pakistani design, reflecting the
identity of Pakistani men and women
in the twenty-first century.

Deepak Perwani

Photography by Tapu Javeri

Photography courtesy of Denis Simachev

Denis Simachev

If Denis Simachev was American, he would be the designer for the second generation of *The Sopranos*, the children that leave the mafia ghetto behind with a look that represents a fusion of the rakish, luxurious gangster type with the carefree style of the street. A trendy and underground appearance resulting from the combination of native aesthetic references and the magnetism of urban gangs.

This Moscow-born designer received extensive training in textile design and graphic arts in his native country, far from Central Saint Martins, a school which, in his case, proved unnecessary for demonstrating his abundant talent and gifts. It wasn't long before his unusual vision began to draw attention. Among the many awards he has received, first prize in the Smirnoff International Fashion Awards in 1999 and first prize for national designers in the Step into the Future competition stand out. In 2001, he started his own label, Denis Simachev. The following year he was already presenting his collections on runways in Paris, and a little later in Milan, in what has proven to be a brilliant career.

In part, the success of this respected designer resides in his looking to the streets of his native country and fashioning a sophisticated look out of original elements: leather, gold, pre-Revolution imperial objects, all joined in an incongruent, artless manner. His stance toward life and art embodies the pride of belonging to a country with a rich historical and cultural legacy and has successfully asserted itself in the international arena.

Photography courtesy of Denis Simachev

Sketch courtesy of Denis Simachev

Above, sketch and design with leather collar, a material which Denis Simachev manipulates with mastery. To the right, a creation from the Spring/Summer 2007 collection in which the designer pays homage to Sunday afternoon games of dominos played with his friends.

Photography courtesy of Denis Simachev

- What inspires you?

Everything. And that's all there is to it.

- What is your dream as a designer?

My dream is to get away to the Dominican Republic and design the uniform for the national swimming team.

- What has been the most important achievement of your career?

A fast and effective promotion track.

- How important are trends?

Trends are not important at all. The main thing is to be a good man.

- Fashion has always reflected a certain era. What does fashion reflect in the twenty-first century?

It reflects a global catastrophe.

- What book would you recommend to every fashion designer?

Pinocchio is an essential book.

Denis Simachev

Nizhniy Susalnyi Side Street, 5, build. 5A

105064 Moscow

Russia

studio@denissimachev.com/www.denissimachev.com

Denis Simachev

Photography courtesy of Denis Simachev

Eley Kishimoto

Photography by Kumi Saito

Eley Kishimoto

Eley Kishimoto is the intelligent combination of the United Kingdom and Japan. The happy communion of English pragmatism and Japanese color. The unexpected outcome of an encounter between disparate influences that miraculously converges to form a new, indivisible aesthetic. Unique. What first grabs one's attention in the garments of Eley Kishimoto is the meticulous graphic quality of the prints, although the cut is the foundation of the designs, the substrate on which the print shapes volumes, pleats and forms.

Mark Eley and Wakako Kishimoto met while they were both students. Mark was born in the south of Wales and studied at the University of Brighton, while Wakako was born in Japan and studied at Central Saint Martins. In 1992, they started their own textile company, and since then their graphic work has covered numerous walls, garments and accessories, giving them a unique, unanticipated quality. Alexander McQueen, Hussein Chalayan, Yves Saint Laurent and Marc Jacobs are some of the designers who have chosen the graphic creations of Eley Kishimoto to appear on their garments.

The prints of Eley Kisimoto began to invade their own collections in 2004. The result was work with strong echoes of op art, Russian Constructivism and psychedelic aesthetics, all rife with arresting combinations and cuts evocative of Japanese attire. From there, the two have continued to advance in what appears to be the contradictory direction of studied improvisation, where the retro horizon of the 70s emerges as the improvised landscape of their creation. A fusion rich in influences and free of the folkloric weight of facile multiculturalism. A vibrant, throbbing hybridization.

Photography by Kumi Saito

Photography by Kumi Saito

Images from the Spring/Summer 2008
collection in which the Eley Kishimoto
duo successfully balances diverse colors
and opposing prints and transports us
back to the amusing 80s.

Photographies by Kumi Saito

- What inspires you?

Inspiration in our interpretation comes in the form of day-to-day living. We do not have the luxury of switching inspiration on and off, as the creative pressures we are under constantly expect us to manifest new ideas continuously. Living life in such a way is very fortunate, and to have daily creative opportunities presented to us is a pleasure. Using notions of normality as inspiration comes naturally.

- What is your dream as designers?

To be happy and motivated, to be positively praised for our efforts and to have longevity with integrity.

- What has been the most important achievement of your career?

Every season we feel satisfied that we have completed a new collection and fulfilled the commercial desires of being responsible and producing. This has been a constant achievement up to this point.

- How important are trends?

For followers of fashion, I presume they are very important, but we hope to think that we are participating to creating trends, as we do not actively pursue the desire to follow them.

- Fashion has always reflected a certain era. What does fashion reflect in the twenty-first century?

Twenty-first century fashion is a mixture of everything.

Eley Kishimoto
215 Lyham Road
London SW2 5PY
United Kingdom
www.eleykishimoto.com

Photography by Kumi Saito

Sketch courtesy of Kishimoto

Sketch and garments from the Spring/
Summer 2008 collection in which
designers once again show their mastery
of prints as well as an ensemble vision
fond of detail and one which invests
absolute faith in an exceptional and
highly personal universe.

Photography by Kumi Saito

Sketches courtesy of Kishimoto

Above, sketches from the Spring/
Summer 2008 collection where prints
take center stage again in the hands
of Wakako Kishimoto, a graduate of
Central Saint Martins who specialized
in fashion and printing. To the right,
an ensemble from this collection.

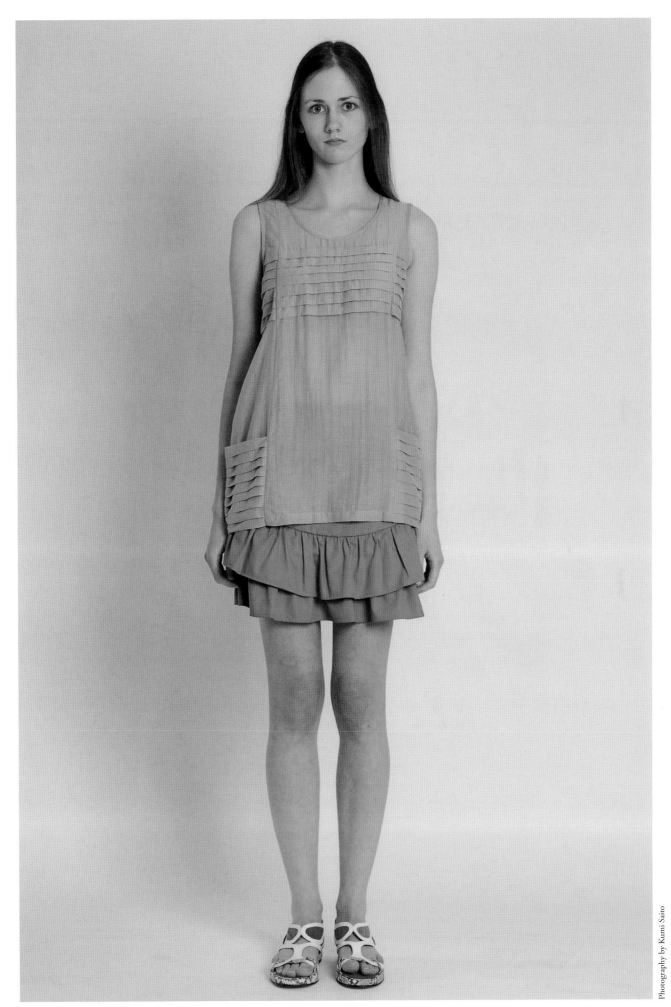

Eley Kishimoto

Photography by Kumi Saito

VILLAGE FÊTE
Spring and Summer 2008 Collection

Chains and chevrons, organization for recreation.
D.I.Y. hyper reality of balloons and bunting superimposed on the field of green.
Shelters of stripes roof over the pride of grit and fluff.
Rosettes on pumpkins, Ribbons on old junks,
Lurid colours on automated horses, A beauty queen with a paper crown.
Thrill for frills make perfect sense till the hired generators are turned off.

Photography by Kumi Saito

Above, the inauguration poster for
"Village Fête," the title of the Spring-
Summer 2008 collection. To the
right, another poster, in this case in
patchwork, and images from backstage.

Photographies by Kumi Saito

Fukuko Ando

Photography by Luigi Migani

Fukuko Ando

If one word could encapsulate the work of this Japanese designer, it would be "poetry": poetry in the way she creates her garments, beginning with the sensation that the textures of the fabrics produce in her fingertips; poetry in the way she extracts from her materials different modes of covering a model while utilizing volumes in the creation of a dress as if she were fashioning a work of pottery.

After completing her studies in literature, she decided to enroll as a fashion design student at the Mode Gakuen vocational school in Nagoya. She later continued her design training at the renowned Chambre Syndicale de la Couture Parisienne, with the goal of understanding Western body forms. And there's no doubt she was successful in this endeavor, as the work of this personal and intimate designer with such big-name firms in French fashion as Christian Dior and Christian Lacroix makes undoubtedly clear.

From these masters she learned the secrets of haute couture, which she then applied to her own vision of fashion. For Fukuko Ando, the creative process signifies an immersion in her own subjective world, a kind of ceremony that involves making garments on a model in front of a mirror so that she can see the evolution of the dress from all perspectives, thereby creating clothes that respect the shape of the human figure.

She is a clear example that the world of fashion reflects not only the spirit of the times but also a personal vision and way of understanding beauty, establishing a dialogue with the fabric on the changing and movable surface of the human form.

Photography by Luigi Migani

Photography by Michael Wayne Plant

Numerous techniques gathered over the
years and adapted for his own purposes
make the creations of Fukuko Ando
unmistakable. Knots, transparencies,
inlaid work and crochet all form part of
his magical universe.

Photography by Michael Wayne Plant

203
Fukuko Ando

- What inspires you?

I'd like to take the Louvre's *Winged Victory of Samothrace* as an example. I can sense the life, the total liberty and energy of this statue. It has a greatness you want to grasp but which eludes you, a movement as full as the wind. The *Victory* symbolizes my desire for a dress that is alive and free through time and space.

- What is your dream as a designer?

Dresses are living beings with a soul, as well as a body. Like the *Winged Victory of Samothrace*, I would like to create dresses that awaken human beings, so that wonderful human souls would open their hearts and reach for the light. This is a prayer.

- What has been the most important achievement of your career?

The Golden Promise (fashion show and performance). Fifteen dancers from the Ballet de l'Opéra National de Paris (including the start dancer, Marie-Agnès Gillot) performed at l'Ecole Nationale Supérieure des Beaux-Arts de Paris in October 2006.

- How important are trends?

My concept of creation is like Madame Madeleine Vionnet. She used to say, "What I made was harmony: an ensemble of shapes and colors that would never change nor age. I wanted only things that would last, not just for a month or a year, but forever."

- Fashion has always reflected a certain era. What does fashion reflect in the twenty-first century?
Love/light now and forever.

- What book would you recommend to every fashion designer?
La chair de la robe, by Madeleine Chapsal, a biography of Madame Madeleine Vionnet.

Fukuko Ando
280, rue Saint-Honoré
75001 Paris
France
www.fukukoando.com

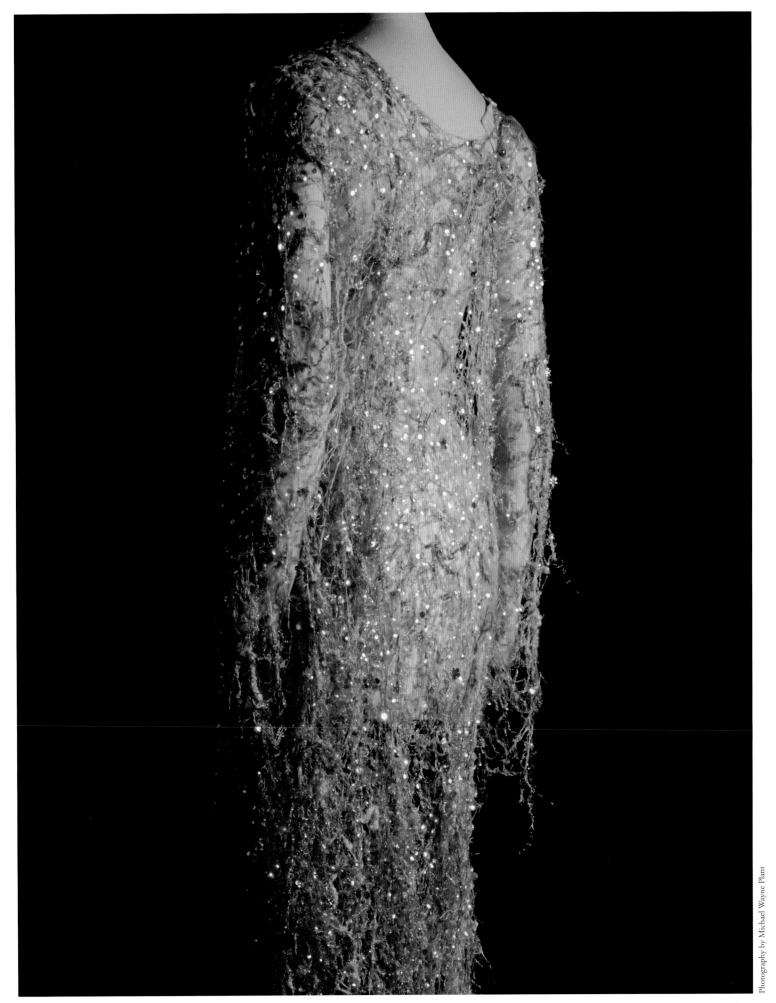

Fukuko Ando

Photography by Michael Wayne Plant

Sketch courtesy of Fukuko Ando

Above, illustration by the designer.
To the right, dress created out of
the covered and open spaces formed
when ribbons of cloth are knotted
together, revealing new qualities and
characteristics of the fabric.

Fukuko Ando

Photography by Michael Wayne Plant

Photography by Michael Wayne Plant

Fukuko Ando

Photography by Michael Wayne Plant

To the left, suit made out of knots
of fabric that form a warp and offer
a glimpse of the figure. Above, suit
consisting of gathers, collected
and bunched together, one of the
characteristic techniques of the
designer.

Photography by Winona Barton

H. Fredriksson

There is something decidedly decadent about the images Helena Fredriksson uses to represent her work: dilapidated buildings in a natural setting that evoke a gray, autumnal, nostalgic landscape. Born in Sweden, Helena soon relocated to New York, where she found a new home in the lively borough of Brooklyn.

Her training is apparent in the attention to volumes, patterns, the simple forms of her garments, and the palette of muted and pure tones she employs. Her designs are uncomplicated, with little showiness or warmth. Ethereal dresses cascade with elegance. Drawings of raw nature illustrate shirts and blouses in a clean, refined manner. Her creations exude sober tranquility.

All of this refers to a kind of dramatic narration. Cinematographic. The women in her photographs, hair worn up in a bun, suggest distance and coldness, a certain strong yet tragic posture, an air of everyday loneliness evinced by her drawings and prints of raw, vacant nature. Elena openly acknowledges the influence of literature and film on her work. For this reason, it's easy to imagine women outfitted in her dresses appearing in a play or a movie, like a character out of Bergman, or one of Ibsen's Nordic heroines.

And it's likely that this sophistication of a northern European woman as depicted on the big screen is one of the reasons for the success of this designer who sells in cities such as Tokyo and New York. This combination of emancipation, humility and intimacy transmitted without affectation has made Helena such a remarkable designer, the creator of an elegant and cultured aesthetic universe.

Photography by Bjarne Jonasson

Sketch courtesy of H. Fredriksson

The Swedish designer uses her knowledge of photography, painting and printing, mediums that appear prominently in all her work, as a way of bringing art closer to fashion. Images from the Spring/Summer 2007 collection.

Photography by Kurt Magnum

H. Fredriksson

- What inspires you?

Art, life, travel, books, music, nature, water, scents, things that are created and made with care, thoughts and change.

- What is your dream as a designer?

To fulfill my concept and vision with an open mind and new inspiration for each collection.

- What has been the most important achievement of your career?

Showing H. Fredriksson for the past six seasons during New York Fashion Week has been great. Continuing to refine the line every season. Collaborating with other great artists.

- How important are trends?

They are, and they aren't. They control consumers and the market to a certain degree, and they can take away from originality and individuality in style. Trends don't affect the design aspect for me when I'm working. I trust my instinct and my eye when creating the collections, and I believe in long-term design aesthetics rather than short-lived trends.

- Fashion has always reflected a certain era. What does fashion reflect in the twenty-first century?

Individuality and strength. It reflects the multifaceted reality we exist in.

- What book would you recommend to every fashion designer?

Wabi-Sabi.

H. Fredriksson
250 West 38th Street #506
New York, NY 10018
United States
www.hfredriksson.com

Photography by Kurt Magnum

Sketch courtesy of H. Fredriksson

The creations of Helena Fredriksson
feature elegant cuts and silhouettes
that allow the body to move with ease.
No rigidity here: all is freedom and
movement. Images from the Spring/
Summer 2007 collection.

H. Fredriksson

Photography by Kurt Magnum

Illustration and design from the Fall/
Winter 2007–2008 season, in which
the multifaceted designer demonstrates
her mastery of highly original volumes
in dresses, coats and skirts.

Sketch courtesy of H. Fredriksson

H. Fredriksson

Photography by Andy Eaton

Photography by Justine/model: Korinna (Models 1)

Helen Storey

The work of Helen Storey places itself somewhere beyond the scope of fashion in a frontier space between art and science, a mysterious, unexplored void that the artist has entered in order to forge a new language, a plastic code by virtue of which science acquires a new, epiphanic meaning.

Fruit of the bond between Helen and her biologist sister was a restlessness that led the designer and artist to comprehend biological processes using the language she knew best: that of fashion. The result was her multi-prize-winning collection Primitive Streak, a visual narration of the process of embryonic development through garments charged with theatricality and optical force. The impact of this collection was so significant that the head of a powerful pharmaceutical company wanted it to be made known throughout the world. A large number of artists, fashion experts, scientists and researchers in the making have praised Helen's work.

Other projects followed, such as Mental and Eye & I, following the same line of aesthetic investigation of the scientific through art under the auspices of the Helen Storey Foundation, a research lab charged with the task of building bridges between science and art.

This designer, with a degree in fashion from the University of Kingston, possesses a thorough command of design, as evidenced by her being named the most innovative designer of 1991 and her nomination as the best British designer by the British Fashion Council. Her passage from the material of fashion to biological fabric can be understood as a glorious evolutionary step, a path toward the disintegration of frontiers.

Photography courtesy of Helen Storey

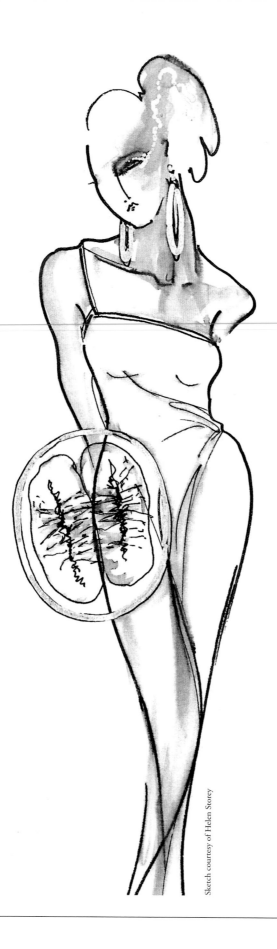

Sketch courtesy of Helen Storey

Image and sketch of the Double DNA Dress. Helen Storey carried out this series in collaboration with her sister, Dr. Kate Storey, the London College of Fashion and her vivid gaze through the microscope.

Photography by Justine/model: Korinna (Models 1)

223
Helen Storey

- Reading about your career, there seem to be two Helens: the fashion entrepreneur with her own brand and the current researcher. What remains of the first one?

The "fashion entrepreneur" thought she should try and contribute more to the world than frocks!

- You mention casual encounters as key moments in the development of your career. How much has luck played a part in the progress of your career?

I'm not sure luck has played a significant part in my career. Looking back, sheer hard work has been at the heart of it. If I had to identify luck in one place, however, it would be meeting my business partner, Caroline Coates, some twenty-three years ago. Ours is an extraordinary relationship and has made my career path a deeply human experience, allowing me to follow and "chance" my instinct and creative ambition beyond where I may have ever gone alone. More often, I'd say luck in general hasn't been around, and a lot of what other people might perceive as progress—artistic or otherwise—has been delivered through the mastery of misfortune. But then again, for anything to retain my interest, there has always got to be something that requires fathoming, or mastering—something must be improved somehow. It's a lot more than the experience of creating alone.

- What is your dream as a designer?

To try to contribute to human advancement in some way.

- What is your dream as a researcher?

As above.

- Fashion has always reflected a certain era. What does fashion reflect in the twenty-first century?

Uncertainty.

- What are you currently researching?

Ways in which to capture solar energy and deliver it in new ways, how to bring scientific, technological and artistic philanthropy into collaborative being for good purpose.

Helen Storey
19 Shuttleworth Road
London SW11 3DH
United Kingdom
www.helenstoreyfoundation.org

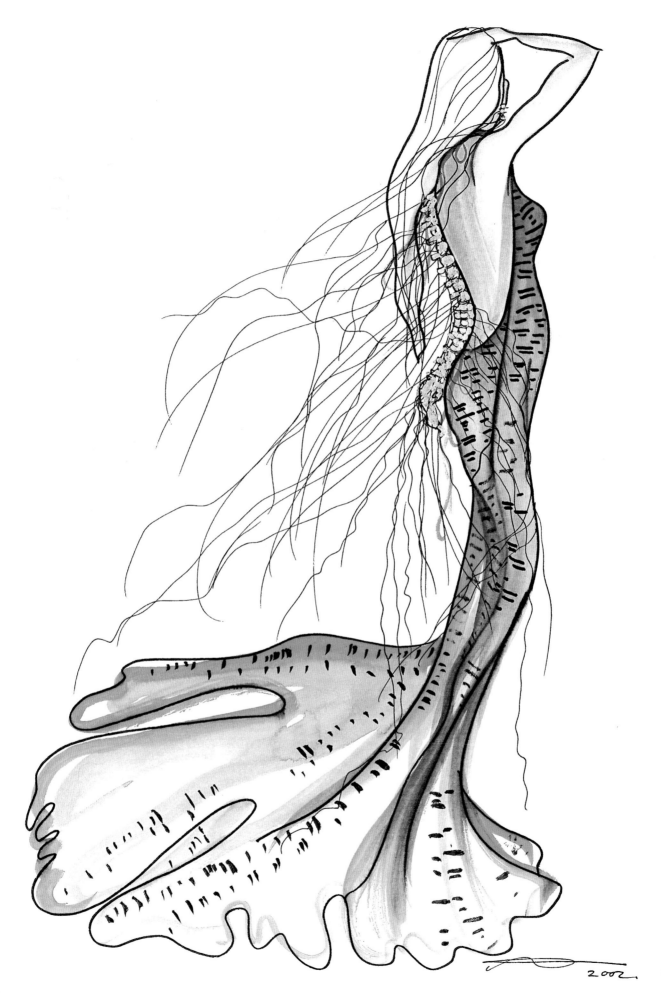

2002

Sketch courtesy of Helen Storey

Helen Storey

Sketches courtesy of Helen Storey

From left to right, sketches of the dresses Closing Neutral Tube Dress, Implantation Dress, and Heart Tubes Fusing Bodice and Skirt. To the right, Spinal Column Dress, in chiffon silk, resin, aluminum fiber and fiber-optic threads.

Photography by Justine/model: Korinna (Models 1)

From left to right, sketches of
Anaphase Dress, Sperm Internal
Structure Dress and White Nerve
Net Dress. To the right, the Anaphase
Dress, in silk, mirror paper, and viscose
fabric.

Sketches courtesy of Helen Storey

Photography by Justine/model: Korinna (Models 1)

Photography by Asger Carlsen

Henrik Vibskov

Henrik Vibskov

Henrik Vibskov was born in Jutland, a peaceful, rural region of Denmark. Everything indicated that the young Henrik would lead a life far from the frenzy of the city until, at the age of twelve, he won a break-dance competition. At that moment, his parents understood that their son wasn't going to sit still for even a second.

And they were right. If a common denominator can be extracted from the diverse artistic career of Henrik, it is the search for change. All of the artistic circles in which this multi-faceted, restless designer moves are marked by a rhythm that beats unstoppably in areas as diverse as film, art, and music. Henrik studied art and design at Central Saint Martins. It wasn't long before he was receiving acclaim from trend-setting magazines that are among the swiftest in snatching up young talent. In the blink of an eye, the work of Henrik Vibskov was appearing in such renowned publications as *The Face, Brutus, Dazed & Confused, I-D* and *Wallpaper.*

Pattern T-shirts, colored socks, checked fabrics, folk-inspired ponchos and colored pants all combine to produce surprising, highly unconventional collections that resist categorization. Henrik is a unique artist that marches energetically to his own drummer in many of his presentations. The creative work of this young artist, however, is not limited to designing clothes. Henrik has exhibited his work in some of the most representative galleries on the five continents. Like a computer virus, his boundless creativity infects the most unexpected places on the planet, all in step with a rhythm marked by the fruitful and contagious torrent of creativity.

Photography by Jacob Langvad

Henrik Vibskov

Photographs by Shoji Fujii

The "Wet Big Shiny Boobies"
collection (Spring/Summer 2008) for
men and women, presented among
breasts which models had to navigate
carefully on the runway.

Photographs by Shoji Fujii

- What inspires you?

Hmm... some of my pieces "belong" to existing people, like a neighbor or a friend or someone, and some just pop up—pop, pop, pop.

- What is your dream as a designer?

It would be fun to have a whole lot of money and make a big pile of clothes and give them to people for free.

- What has been the most important achievement of your career?

That I can merge all my interests, music and art. For the Fantabulous Bicycle Music Factory, we made this installation with bikes that empower music instruments, something like that. The fact that people like that.

- How important are trends?

That's a good question for a job interview at Ralph Lauren.

- Fashion has always reflected a certain era. What does fashion reflect in the twenty-first century?

I have honestly never thought about that.

- The book you would recommend to every fashion designer is...

Where's Wally? The Fantastic Journey.

Henrik Vibskov
Vesterbrogade 69d, St, Baghuset
Copenhagen 1620 V
Denmark
www.henrikvibskov.com

Photography by Shoji Fujii

Photography by Shoji Fujii

The "Black Carrots" collection (Fall/ Winter 2007–2008) for men and women. On this occasion, the Danish designer had the runway strewn with carrots to present a collection that urges the spectator to enter into his own personal world.

Henrik Vibskov

Photography by Shoji Fujii

Open your mind.
Show Spirit

Graphic design by Lissajous

Hikaru Katano

Hikaru Katano

Japan is the cradle of the most innovative fashion designers in recent years, talents that can be characterized by their constant research into textile, technological and aesthetic matters and their cultural contribution to a West always astounded and amazed by what reaches it from the Land of the Rising Sun. Within this panorama, Hikaru Katano, with his Share Spirit label, emerges as something completely different.

After attending Tokyo's prestigious Bunka Fashion College, he set off for England, driven by an urge to see the world and learn English, a language which would allow him to realize his principal passion of traveling and learning about new cultures.

India, Bali, Hong Kong, Morocco, Mongolia, Mexico and Peru are some of the places this designer has visited, collecting traditional garments, jewelry and ideas as sources of inspiration for his own collections. Yet, in terms of symbolism, this also serves as means for appreciating the passage of time, tradition and the richness of cultural heterogeneity. Indeed, his designs are a rare thing in fashion today, representing an avenue of escape in a world in need of ideas and characterized by excessive speed and a frenetic pace.

His Tokyo store is a veritable museum of objects from different parts of the world. Full of history and symbolism, they are a source of sensations and energy fundamental to his creative work, the same energy he seeks to transmit in his collections.

Photography courtesy of Hikaru Katano

Photography courtesy of Hikaru Katano

Above, an image of a nook of his store
in Japan that houses diverse objects
collected by the designer on his travels
which serve as a source of creative
inspiration. To the right, a sketch done
especially for this book.

Hikaru
Katano

Sketch courtesy of Hikaru Katano

241
Hikaru Katano

- What inspires you?

Traveling all over the world and meeting people, especially different races. I get incentive from their different sense of values and culture. Pure things born in the world of nature are what most inspire me.

- What is your dream as a designer?

To spend the richest time—making clothes is the most free and enjoyable for me—not to succeed in the fashion business world. I could say it is artistic clothes. I have been trying to spend ten years making just one piece of clothing.

- What has been the most important achievement of your career?

To continue working as a designer for twenty years, the people who support me and "connection."

- How important are trends?

I suppose trends are needed by the world. My "trends" are spiritual.

- Fashion has always reflected a certain era. What does fashion reflect in the twenty-first century?

More artistic clothes are needed by people, and I wish it could be. I feel the recent fashion scene pursues too much business and profit. Philosophy and ideas have to be needed by fashion companies and designers, and it becomes strong message to people.

- What book would you recommend to every fashion designer?

First Seen—Portraits of the World's Peoples. Avedon—Photographs, 1947–1977.

Hikaru Katano
14-10 Hachiyama-cho, Shibuya-ku
Tokyo 150-0035
Japan
www.sharespirit.jp

Open your mind.

Share Spirit

Graphic design by Lissajous

Hikaru Katano

Photography courtesy of Igor Chapurin

Igor Chapurin

A witness to the Soviet change, Igor Chapurin belongs to a new generation of Russian designers searching for an identity of their own in the fashion universe, and there is little doubt that their search is proving fruitful.

Born near the Estonian border, he is one of the most celebrated Russian designers working today. He garnered attention fashioning dresses for the Miss Europe, Miss World and Miss Universe pageants and, thanks to the international reach of these contests, gradually accumulated a prestige that resulted in his being the first Russian fashion designer to have a show in a Paris.

His stellar year was 1998, when his haute couture collection won the Golden Mannequin Prize awarded by the Russian Association of Haute Couture and he was also awarded the Style Prize given by *Harper's Bazaar* magazine.

Alongside his fashion career, he has been involved in a variety of activities that have only served to enrich his brilliant trajectory as a designer. These projects include producing the wardrobe for the production of *Madam Lioneli* in London's Royal Albert Hall, the creation of the line of products for the Chapurincasa firm in 2003, and the children's line Chapurin Child in 2005. Additionally, he was responsible for designing the set and scenic wardrobe of the Bolshoi Theatre for works of classical dance by such composers as Stravinsky and Tchaikovsky, an honor given only to an elite few. The spectacle of Russian fashion has only just begun, and the world is anxious to witness it.

Photography courtesy of Igor Chapurin

In the legendary L'Imperiale lobby of the Westin Hotel and Hall Soufflot in Paris, the Russian designer presented his Fall/Winter 2007–2008 collection, with a combination of leather and fur in an atmosphere that transported the spectator back to the forties.

Photography courtesy of Igor Chapurin

Photography courtesy of Igor Chapurin

- What inspires you?

The sources of my inspiration are my personal hobbies and passions which I put on the paper. It could be the theme of a ballet dancer, either the troubled revolution through the image of the daughter of Nicholas II, Anastasia, or the image of a Nabokov's heroine, Lolita. In the last collection, I tried to imagine how the Aztecs and Maya would look if they were the aliens who came back in our twenty-first century.

- What is your dream as a designer?

I dream to create the interior of the avialiners (airplanes).

- What has been the most important achievement of your career?

The dream of my life has been realized. I`ve been dreaming about that, but I was afraid at the same time. Now I create the decorations and costumes for the ballet of the Bolshoi Theatre in Moscow.

- How important are trends?

Trends define society; I only create the clothes. It's not up to me to govern fashion trends. Modern fashion is less the proportions, more the elements which touch the person, their nervous receptors. That is why the latest trends are seen in accessories.

- Fashion has always reflected a certain era. What does fashion reflect in the twenty-first century?

My time is crazy, dynamic, active, aggressive. It requires very simple, clear forms. Fashion today is very rational: feminine silhouettes combine with harsh, almost masculine fabrics, silk with rude wool, delicate lace and brutal leather. The functionality of clothing is very important today. A woman needs to change clothes depending on the situation. A day-to-day dress should be easily transformed into a cocktail dress, adding the right accents with the help of accessories and jewelry.

- What book would you recommend to every fashion designer?

Alexander Vasiliev's *The History of Fashion.*

Igor Chapurin

21 Savinnskaya embankment

119435 Moscow

Russia

www.chapurin.com

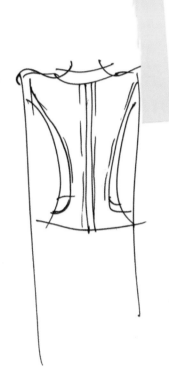

CHAPURIN

Тихофтьфа

Sketch courtesy of Igor Chapurin

Photography courtesy of Igor Chapurin

Oversized sleeves and mini-dresses
of fur and leather, as can be seen in
both images, were the unquestionable
protagonists of the Fall/Winter
2007–2008 collection that Igor
Chapurin presented with much success
in the French capital.

Photography courtesy of Igor Chapurin

251
Igor Chapurin

Photography by Carin Verbauggen

Ilja Visser

Ilja Visser studied fashion design in Arnhem. After that, she moved to Milan, where she learned the ins and outs of the business before launching a label bearing her name in 2005.

The work of this Dutch designer is known for and recognized by the feminine elegance and sophistication of her suits and dresses, all delicately cut and made with excellent materials such as silk, wool and crepe, relaxed creations consisting of tulle and pastel tones that coordinate an urban, distinguished woman without frills.

The lack of pomp and complication characteristic of her garments is studied and measured. It involves a simplicity sought after (and found) by a designer interested in making comfortable, casual clothes without having to sacrifice elegance. There are no unnecessary accessories. Looking at Ilja's clothes, one is assured that harmony and simplicity are the only things needed for a woman who wants her clothes to beautify her quietly.

What this comes down to is an exceptionally successful attempt to make the nonstop movement of a cosmopolitan woman feminine, distinguished and comfortable, in balance with the rapidly changing rhythm of big Western cities, a new placement of the feminine in the public sphere.

Photography by RVDA

Sketches by the Dutch designer who,
prior to founding her own label,
worked for designers of the stature
of Donna Karan and María Cornejo
creating fashion collections for women.

Sketch courtesy of Ilja Visser

Sketch courtesy of Ilja Visser

- What inspires you?

People, buildings, colors that have been used oddly, the way a large sweater is worn by someone who is too small for it. It can be anything—anything that's intriguing by just looking at it.

- What is your dream as a designer?

I would like to have my own stores in New York, Los Angeles, Japan and Paris.

- What has been the most important achievement of your career?

There's no specific achievement. Every day, getting closer to the creation of a steady foundation for my company is a great achievement.

- How important are trends?

Trends are very important to people, because they give them the choice whether to bond with or be different from others. Both ways can make people feel good. For me personally, trends don't have anything to do with designing.

- Fashion has always reflected a certain era. What does fashion reflect in the twenty-first century?

I think it's very likely that two ways of reflection will be further developed. One is more future-minded—think high-speed, fast and furious, metallic cold look. But I also believe people definitely will long for craft industry. Individuality is a very obvious phenomenon; people are becoming increasingly estranged from each other. At the same time, they are becoming what I like to call "clones" of each other. And to make it a bit more complicated, they are becoming clones while still thinking of ways to stay different in all sorts of ways. Naturally, fashion plays a big part in this.

- What book would you recommend to every fashion designer?

Several! I read *The House of Gucci*, by Sarah Gay Forden, in one go, but *War Paint*, by Lindy Woodhead, and *Queen of Fashion*, by Caroline Weber, are also interesting and pleasant to read. *Who Moved My Cheese?*, by Spencer Johnson, is a great book in general, whoever you are!

Ilja Visser
Rokin 140-142
1012 LE Amsterdam
The Netherlands
www.iljavisser.com

Photography by Peter Stigter

257
Ilja Visser

Images from the Fall/Winter 2008–
2009 season. Except for sporadic
brushstrokes of pure sky blue, as in
the garments on these pages, the color
black was predominant.

Photography by Peter Stigter

Photography by Peter Stigter

Photography by Peter Stigter

The Fall/Winter 2008–2009 collection
demonstrates some of the designer's
most characteristic features: a chic
simplicity and a modern, very feminine
image joined with an always-present
elegant sophistication.

Photography by Peter Stigter

Isabela Capeto

© Marcio Madeira

Isabela Capeto

The garments of Isabela Capeto exude delicacy, a simple and subtle sensibility reflected in work carried out with extreme care. Patchworks and embroidery tenderly border her garments; bows, lace and other elements of traditional dressmaking evoke quality handcrafted domestic attire. Isabela depicts a modern woman that seeks to live in harmony with her surroundings, free of the stresses generated by large Western cities where the triumph of the functional results in spiritless garments adapted to an accelerated pace.

In the designs of Isabela Capeto, space is always left for details. This care is apparent not only in the finish, but also in a manual production process carried out by seamstresses with natural fabrics and in compliance with the standards of social responsibility, making clear the designer's firm commitment to the reality of her surroundings.

Born in Brazil, Isabela studied at the Accademia di Moda in Florence. She is considered one of the most important fashion designers in her country—an honor she has earned not by yielding to the trends set on international catwalks, but by doing what she knows best: creating romantic garments that make a woman feel beautiful and natural.

For this reason, her designs appear in the best stores and magazines in the world. For this reason, her label continues to grow at a meteoric pace. And for this reason, she is considered one of the most relevant figures in her native Brazil—a Brazil that exports its own idea of a woman far removed from clichés, a woman that avoids aesthetic pretense, natural and coquettish, comfortable with who she is.

Photography by Carolina Dias Leite

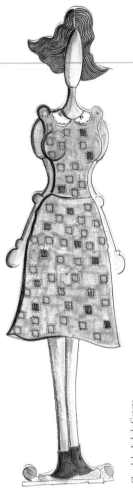

Sketch by Isabela Capeto

Sketches and images from the Spring/
Summer 2008 collection "Nature,"
in which Isabela Capeto reflects on
the return to simplicity, creating a
sensation of naturalness, pleasantness,
and calm through authentic falls and
pure materials.

© Marcio Madeira

- What inspires you?

Everything—friends, trips, magazines, books, food, exhibitions...

- What is your dream as a designer?

My dream is to have many organized workstations in different countries, each one specialized in a different thing (embroidery, sewing, etc.).

- What has been the most important achievement of your career?

Being able to sell my clothes to many different countries.

- How important are trends?

I think the important thing is to try to be connected to everything. Trends are a consequence of this.

- Fashion has always reflected a certain era. What does fashion reflect in the twenty-first century?

Versatility.

- What book would you recommend to every fashion designer?

Any book about the Dadaism movement.

Isabela Capeto
Rua General Dionísio, 57
22271-050 Rio de Janeiro, RJ
Brazil
www.isabelacapeto.com.br

© Marcio Madeira

267
Isabela Capeto

Above, another image from the
"Nature" collection (Spring/Summer
2008). To the right, details of the
garments, highlighting the care and
meticulous, assiduous craftsmanship
that go into all of Isabela's work.

© Marcio Madeira

Photographies courtesy of Isabela Capeto

270
Isabela Capeto

© Marcio Madeira

© Marcio Madeira

Designs from the Fall/Winter 2007–
2008 collection entitled "Outsider,"
which vindicates freedom of creation
beyond any regulation, beyond any
limit. The only requirement is to make
a woman feel comfortable with herself.

Photography by Amy Trost

272
Jens Laugesen

Jens Laugesen

"Chance is not, nor can it be, anything more than the unknown cause of an unknown effect," Voltaire once stated. The part of a designer's work that revolves around the concept of "hybrid" cannot be mere chance, but perhaps it could be the result of causality. Danish designer Jens Laugesen's eager interest in microbiology, genetic modification and hybridization—so fitting at the outset of the new millennium, as they are fields in which everything gets combined, reconstructed and reinvented—has been apparent in much of his work since the outset of his career. In fact, his original plan was to study microbiology and specialize in genetics—that is, until fashion crossed his path. What he did, though, was capture the spirit of his original passion and bring it to his new-found one, creating collections situated in technological and futuristic landscapes with designs that approach the conceptual and yet speak to our everyday lives.

In 1987, he moved to Paris, where he studied haute couture at the Chambre Syndicale de la Couture Parisienne, going on in 1994 to earn a master's degree in management from the Institut Française de la Mode. He worked for various fashion houses in the French capital until, in 2000, he decided to go to London to pursue another master's, this time in women's wear fashion at Central Saint Martins College. His graduation collection was a big hit, signaling the beginning of a career of countless accomplishments and prizes, among them the 2003 New Generation Award given by the British Fashion Council, which made him an indispensable figure at London Fashion Week.

Since then, his work has not gone unnoticed by anyone, and even less by the multitude of specialty magazines that laud every one of his collections.

Photography by Jean Françoise Carly

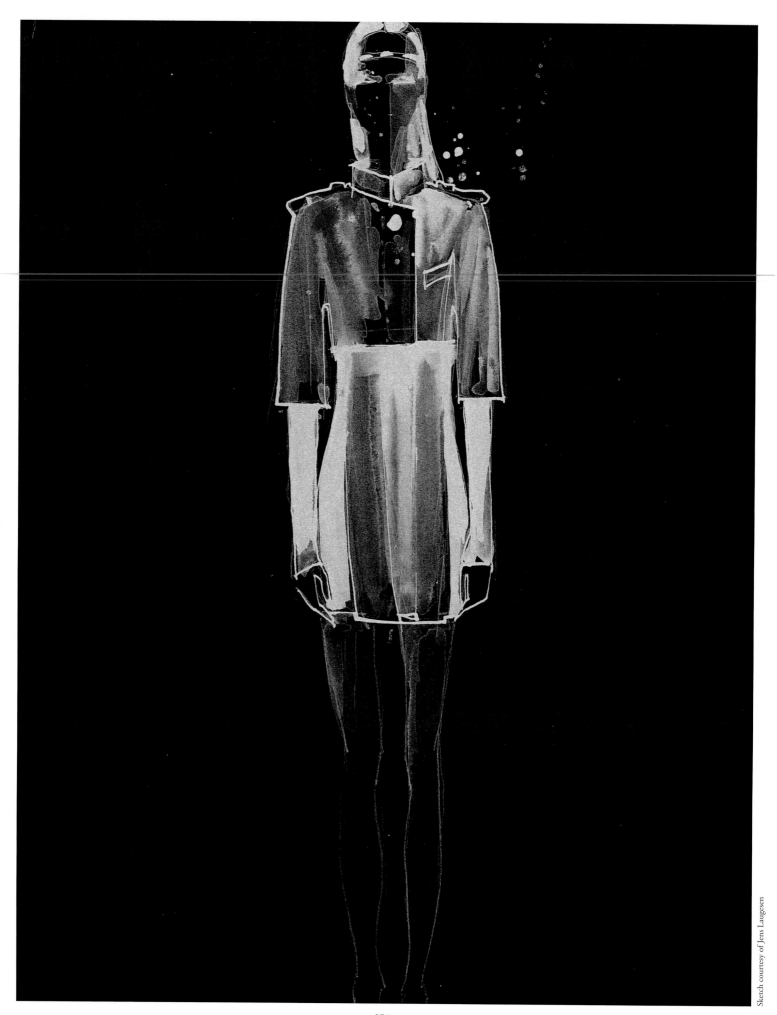

Sketch courtesy of Jens Laugesen

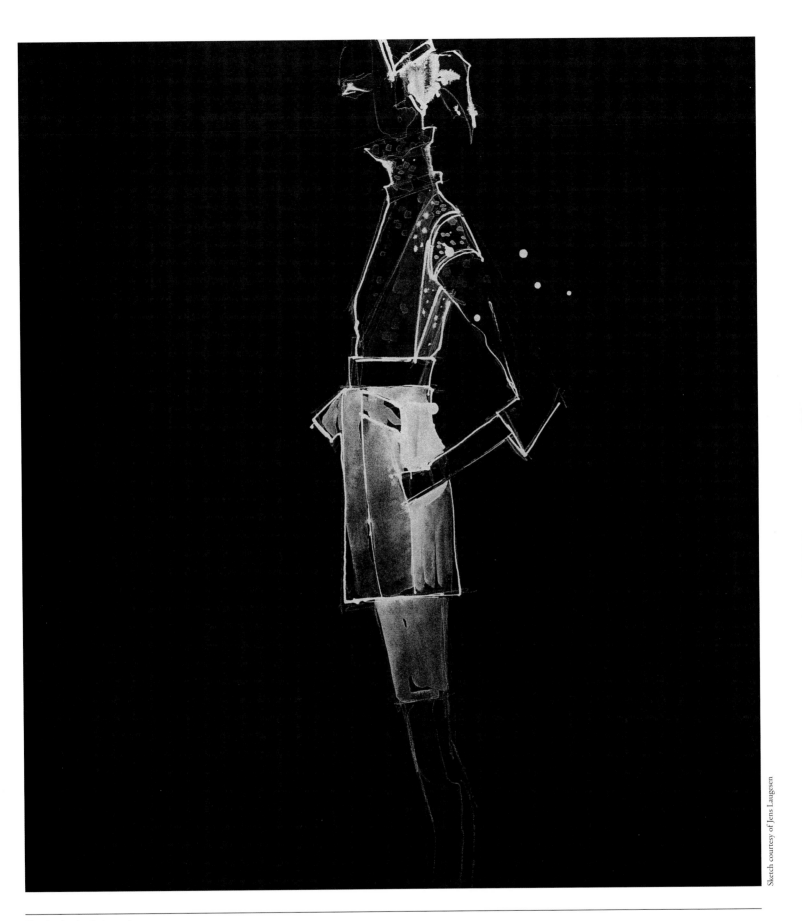

Sketch courtesy of Jens Laugesen

Sketches by the designer that,
beginning with faint traces, show the
most characteristic features of his work:
structurally minimalist silhouettes
opposite complex details, which
combine to make his garments unique.

- What inspires you?

I am inspired by objects and ideas I discover from the past, especially vintage garments that reflect a different aesthetic. I think that, since postmodernism, everything has been done in fashion, so today it is about how a designer reappropriates found objects and turns them into a personal statement.

- What is your dream as a designer?

Initially, I wanted to study genetics and research cloning and genetic manipulation, but I decided it would be better for me to unite the artistic and scientific sides of my nature. I found fashion to be an area where I could fuse scientific and structural thinking with intuitive creativity. It is my dream to become a truly modern design/fashion house, reflecting my hybrid nature as a person and the work I do as a designer.

- What has been the most important achievement of your career?

On a personal level, my most important achievement has been to redefine my profile as a designer. On a professional level, I think the long list of awards and prizes I have won since graduation from Central Saint Martins in 2002 represents my biggest achievement thus far.

- How important are trends?

For me, trends can be considered a commercial necessity invented by the industry in order to convince consumers to buy seasonally. I think that trends are really important for sales, but it is more about finding your own personal statement, in order to put forward an ideology that allows you to achieve longevity in your career.

- Fashion has always reflected a certain era. What does fashion reflect in the twenty-first century?

For me, twenty-first century fashion has to become modern in a way that reflects the hybrid, recomposed nature of our culture. I think that at the turn of any century, there is a radical shift in aesthetics and ways of thinking, and so I am looking for new signs of this "new kind of modernism" that everybody knows will follow postmodernism.

- What book would you recommend to every fashion designer?

I also work as a tutor at Saint Martins, and I never advise different students in the same way. I think all students and designers are individual, and it is through cultivating the individual that everybody becomes unique. However, I think the most important books were never visual, but philosophical or spiritual instead. These ideas are what moves our personality and creates these shifts that are so crucial to our development.

Jens Laugesen
8 Lauburn Street
London E2 8AY
United Kingdom
www.jenslaugesen.com

Photography by Chris Moore

Photography by Amy Trost

Jeremy Laing

Born in Toronto, Jeremy Laing spent the majority of his childhood on a military base. Instead of becoming interested in weapons, however, he chose a far different path in life. His mother, a master of dressmaking and arts and crafts, was the one who indirectly instilled her son with a passion for the needle and thread. At age thirteen, Laing was already an expert tailor.

His destiny was set: an European exchange led him to study at Westminster University in London and then to work with one of the most creative and charismatic designers of this decade, Alexander McQueen.

His talent for making patterns and coupling pieces, for employing fabrics and for the architectural construction of each and every one of his garments manifests itself in a holistic vision which he refers to as "organic." He conceives of fashion as a union of elements that, when brought together, take on meaning and result in the perfect garment. It is no surprise that he is great admirer of designers such as Balenciaga and Madame Vionnet.

The architectural ideation of his garments and the perfect finishes, the feminine look and, more than anything, the uncommon way in which his designs fall over the figure have resulted in his work appearing in the world's top fashion magazines, all of this without losing even a sliver of the spontaneity that characterized his early work while remaining firmly grounded in the city of his birth.

Photography by Frank Griggs

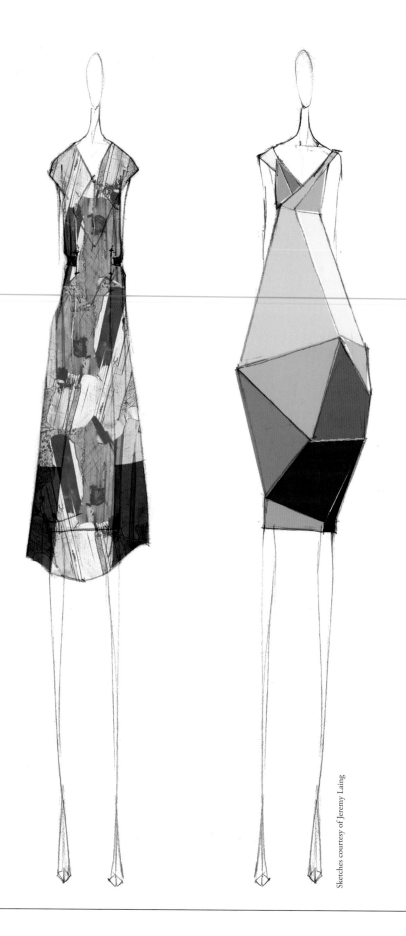

Sketches courtesy of Jeremy Laing

Spring/Summer 2008 collection of the
Canadian designer with suits that embody
his uncommon architectural sensibility,
elaborated in materials such as silk. For
the printing of some of the garments, he
enjoyed, in addition, the collaboration of
the artist Karen Azoulay.

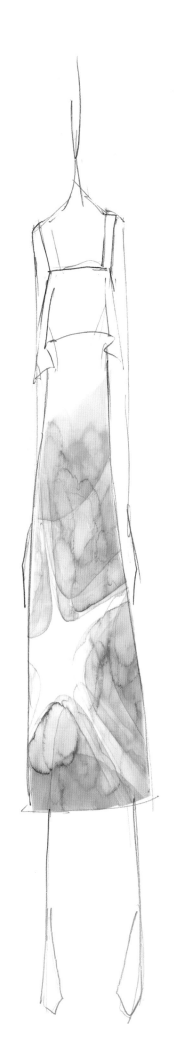

Sketch courtesy of Jeremy Laing

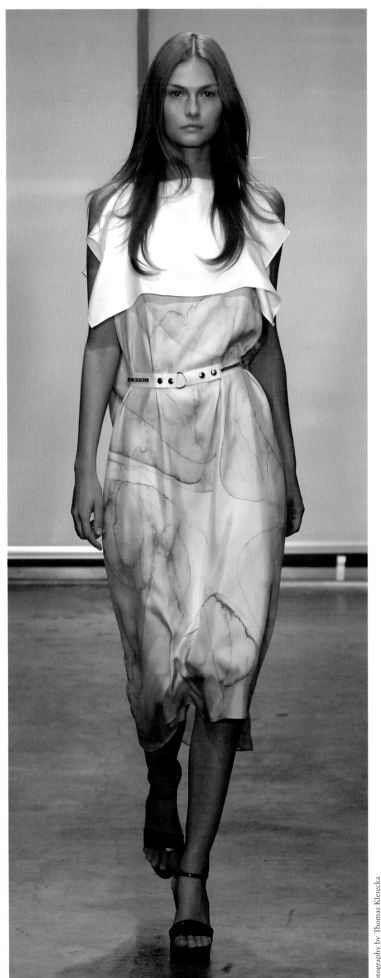

Photography by Thomas Kletecka

- What inspires you?

I'm inspired by the natural world, the couture tradition, working with fabric and materials, the geometries of pattern-making, and—perhaps most importantly—the body and the fitting process.

- What is your dream as a designer?

My goals are to continue evolving my craft, to grow organically and with credibility, to maintain control, to continue to collaborate with other artists and designers, and to expand my product lines. I can't wait to do menswear, for selfish reasons.

- What has been the most important achievement of your career?

The most important achievement in my career has yet to happen.

- How important are trends?

Obviously, from a commercial perspective, trends are important, much more important than specific trendy things, which formally don't matter at all. What does matter is their trendiness. From a conceptual standpoint, which could itself be described as a trendy one, trends are reductive and banal and, therefore, necessary in reaching a majority. Being more interested in the form and in the creative process, as well as tight distribution and the development of a consistent signature, I find that trends have only a small bearing on my work.

- Fashion has always reflected a certain era. What does fashion reflect in the twenty-first century?

Fashion is a product of the late nineteenth and the twentieth century. It didn't exist before then, at least not in the state that we know it today. This is not the case with fashionableness, which has existed throughout history, or at least for as long as humans have been interested in status and the creation and maintenance of social hierarchies.

Twenty-first century fashion reflects the state of advanced capitalism that produces it, and it is not limited to clothing and luxury goods. All production is subject to, and yet depends on, the whims of fashion. This includes paintings, music, film, buildings, fast food, whole technologies, even ideas. Fashion drives everything that can be consumed.

- What book would you recommend to every fashion designer?

The Arcades Project, by Walter Benjamin, as well as *Conspicuous Consumption*, by Thorstein Veblen.

Jeremy Laing
1342 Queen Street West, Suite 3
Toronto, ON M6K 1L4
Canada
www.jeremylaing.com

Photography by Amy Trost

Jeroen van Tuyl

Photography by Peter Stigter

Jeroen van Tuyl

Cultural heterogeneity is beyond a doubt the source of some of the most interesting artists and projects. Jeroen van Tuyl, a fashion designer of Indian origin from Rotterdam who presents his creations on the prestigious Paris catwalk, is a shining example of this. After graduating in 1998 from Hogeschool voor de Kunsten in Arnhem, he founded the Van-TUYL DeROOIJ along with his partner Edwin de Rooij, garnering considerable success with the presentation of their first two collections: "New Entity" (Spring/Summer 2000) and "Klapstoel" (Fall/Winter 2000-2001). In 2001, now working alone, Jeroen founded his own label, the evolution of which has made him one of the great promises of Dutch and European men's fashion. Additionally, he has worked for some of the most interesting designers of men's fashion on the European scene, including Dirk Bikkembergs and Joe Casely-Hayford.

From the beginning of his career, he has shown his work in Paris and has always appeared on the calendar of Men's Fashion Week in the French capital, in addition to forming part of the French Federation of Fashion and of Ready-to-Wear of Couturiers and Fashion Designers.

Jeroen is gifted with the ability to combine the best of tailoring with street fashion and the idiosyncrasies of his own personal universe. Since his first collection, "Sherp," he has been perfecting his style and honing his professionalism, always faithful to what brought him to notice in the first place: sound dressmaking, polished cuts, and a very "street" modernity with a hint of surprise, qualities which always dazzle the specialized European press.

Photography by Dale Grant

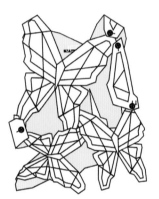 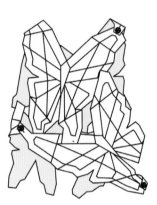 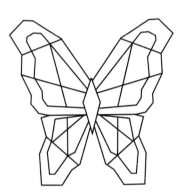 

Sketch courtesy of Jeroen van Tuyl

Images from the Spring/Summer 2007
collection: "Transformer." In the image
on the right, a design by the Dutch
designer consisting of black wool
pants and an original butterfly top of
interlaced leather.

287
Jeroen van Tuyl

Photography by Peter Stigter

- What inspires you?

The past and the future. In my work, I always start with archetype classical garments. In addition to this, there is my fascination for the future: the speed of the way things change, the possibilities with new technologies. I am very curious about the possibilities the future brings, like new techniques. On the other hand, I really like nostalgia, purity, tradition and craftsmanship. I work with classical garments and with classical fabrics.

- What is your dream as a designer?

My dream is the possibility to explore and work in all the fields of which the senses can be approached; so it's not only fashion and design, sight and texture, but also sound and smell. I would also like to work in different disciplines. For example, I already made a short animation movie with a photographer, I want to make sounds for my fashion shows, and I've worked and discussed with an architect friend about special projects.

- What has been the most important achievement of your career?

I still have to achieve. I am proud of a lot of stuff, but I still want to do a lot.

- How important are trends?

I normally do not follow trends in general, but there are some trends you have to know just to be able to choose to work with them or simply to avoid them.

- What book would you recommend to every fashion designer?

Neuromancer (1984), by William Gibson. It was a sort of dictionary for the future.

Jeroen van Tuyl
Puntegaalstraat 267
3024EB Rotterdam
The Netherlands
www.jeroenvantuyl.com

Jeroen van Tuyl

Photography by Peter Stigter

Photography by Peter Stigter

Designs from the Fall/Winter 2007–
2008 collection, titled "Dragontech,"
featuring sweaters, duffle coats and
raincoats, all summed up in the design
of an unusual dragon, appearing in
these images on a sweater and a scarf.

Jeroen van Tuyl

Photography by Peter Stigter

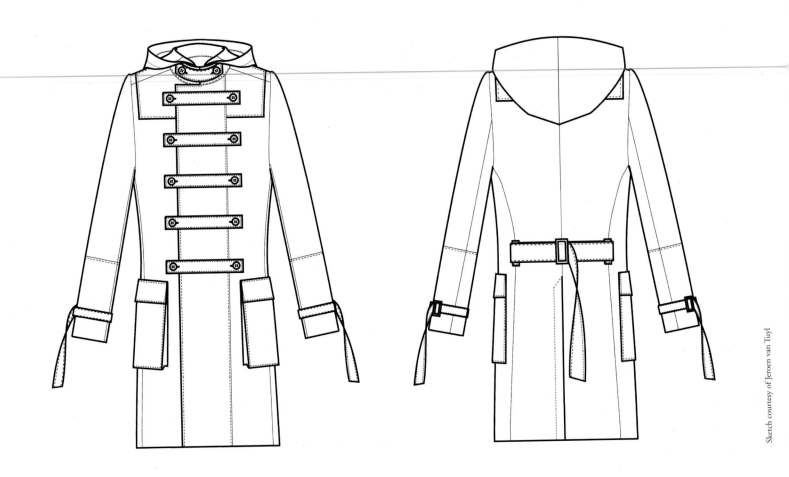

Sketch courtesy of Jeroen van Tuyl

Fall/Winter 2007–2008 collection.
Above, the design specifications for the
wool duffle coat that appears in the
image, with exterior bellows pockets
and hood. Over her face, the model
wears a mask that gives the collection
its name: Dragontech.

Jeroen van Tuyl

Photography by Peter Stigter

Photography by Paul Bliss

Joe Casely-Hayford

Joe Casely-Hayford

Joe Casely-Hayford quickly realized he wasn't going to continue in the academic tradition of his Ghanaian family. As a child, he was fascinated by the urban tribes of the 60s and 70s—by their aesthetic identities, their personalized composition of style. For this reason, at the age of just fifteen, he was creating garments out of the remnants of second-hand clothes.

This taste for the mechanics of clothing and the composition of an outfit came to fruition in his intense tailoring training in London. Subsequent training in art history and studies at Central Saint Martins rounded out his education.

Joe's technical training has endowed him with the skill of making nearly perfect suits. His masterful designing of patterns and an engineering-like knowledge for assembling the pieces of unique, custom-made combinations are astounding. Add to this a special sensibility for capturing styles that originate on the street and you have the best of English tailoring at the service of a modern vision. The result: a rakish, elegant and impeccable look—or, in other words, the purest Joe Casely-Hayford style.

It is therefore no accident that this designer has dressed musicians such as Lou Reed, Neneh Cherry, Liam Gallagher and the members of U2, as his garments exude a dark, distinguished, rock-and-roll charm, a refined yet dangerous club look. Joe achieves these accomplishments by overcoming the rigidity of traditional suits, endowing them with a certain chaos. The union of tailoring tradition and youth culture. Exquisite, elegant suits cut by the hand of a true master.

Photography by Dan Annet

Designs from the Fall/Winter 2004–
2005 collection. To the left, high waist
mini-short and mini-jacket of brilliant
tweed. To the right, also in bright
material, a black trench dress.

Photography by Paul Bliss

Photography by Paul Bliss

- What inspires you?

I am inspired by individualism and creativity. The constraints of Western society make it increasingly difficult for genuine individual expression. I admire those with the courage and conviction to create their own statement, whether this is through literature, art, fashion or music. It's great to be inspired by ideas that aren't necessarily the result of commerce.

- What is your dream as a designer?

As a designer, I dream of a point when we can redefine the creative process and the function of the fashion designer in the twenty-first century. I believe that today there is little purpose in seasonal collections, which become devalued before they reach the stores. All colors are simultaneously in and out of fashion. The role of the "conventional" catwalk system is more or less defunct. I dream of a time when designers can collaborate with scientific laboratories and technicians to make clothes that may not be seasonal, but get closer to fulfilling the requirements of the twenty-first century consumer.

- What has been the most important achievement of your career?

My most important achievement has been designing some original products that have transcended fashion and have become new classics. I think that some of the stage costumes I created for groups like The Clash and U2 have influenced popular culture in some small way.

- How important are trends?

Trends today are more significant than before, but they last for a shorter time. They sometimes have varying degrees of impact within the many social groups that make up the fashion audience. Because the media today has a more powerful influence, an idea can grow from underground to global in a very short period of time and then die just as quickly. In order to become less susceptible to trends, fashion brands are investing more in developing a house signature than being trend-led.

- Fashion has always reflected a certain era. What does fashion reflect in the twenty-first century?

The twenty-first century reflects the best bits of the twentieth century, streamlined and polished up for easy consumption. I think the strongest signature of the twenty-first century is not aesthetic but an increase in our appreciation of quality and fine detail. Postmodernism has homogenized our vision.

- What book would you recommend to every fashion designer?

I would recommend every designer read *Against Nature*, by Huysmans.

Joe Casely-Hayford
19-23 Kingsland Road
London E2 8AA
United Kingdom
www.joecaselyhayford.co.uk

Sketch courtesy of Joe Casely-Hayford

Photography courtesy of Joe Casely-Hayford

Above, image from the Fall/Winter 2003–2004
footwear collection. To the right, designer
specifications for knitwear from the Spring/
Summer 2007 season for the prestigious British
tailor's shop, located at Number One Savile Row,
Gieves & Hawkes, a collection in which Joe
Casely-Hayford collaborated as creative director.

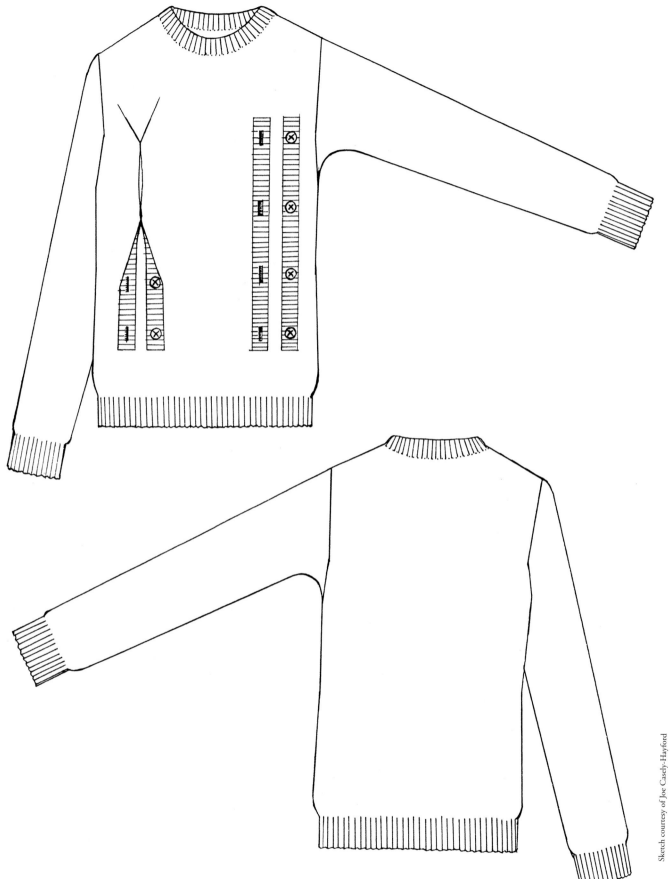

Sketch courtesy of Joe Casely-Hayford

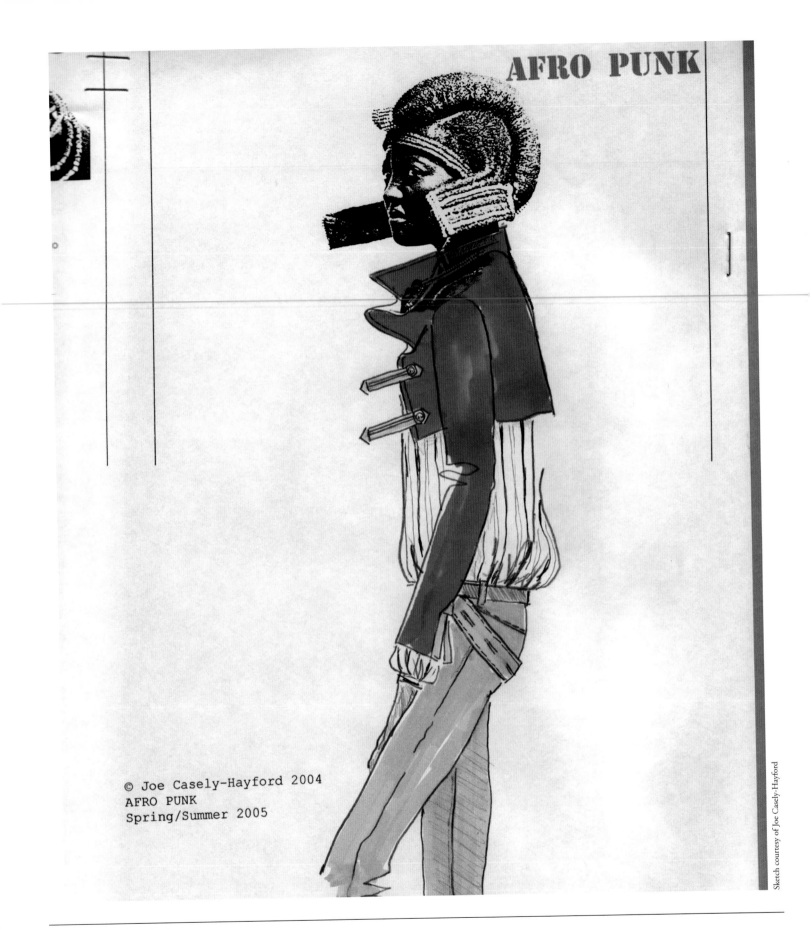

AFRO PUNK

© Joe Casely-Hayford 2004
AFRO PUNK
Spring/Summer 2005

Sketch courtesy of Joe Casely-Hayford

Illustrations from the Spring/Summer
2005 collection "Afro Punk," in which
the designer demonstrates one of
his most characteristic features: the
collision between the most up-to-date,
rebellious identity and the purest
tailoring.

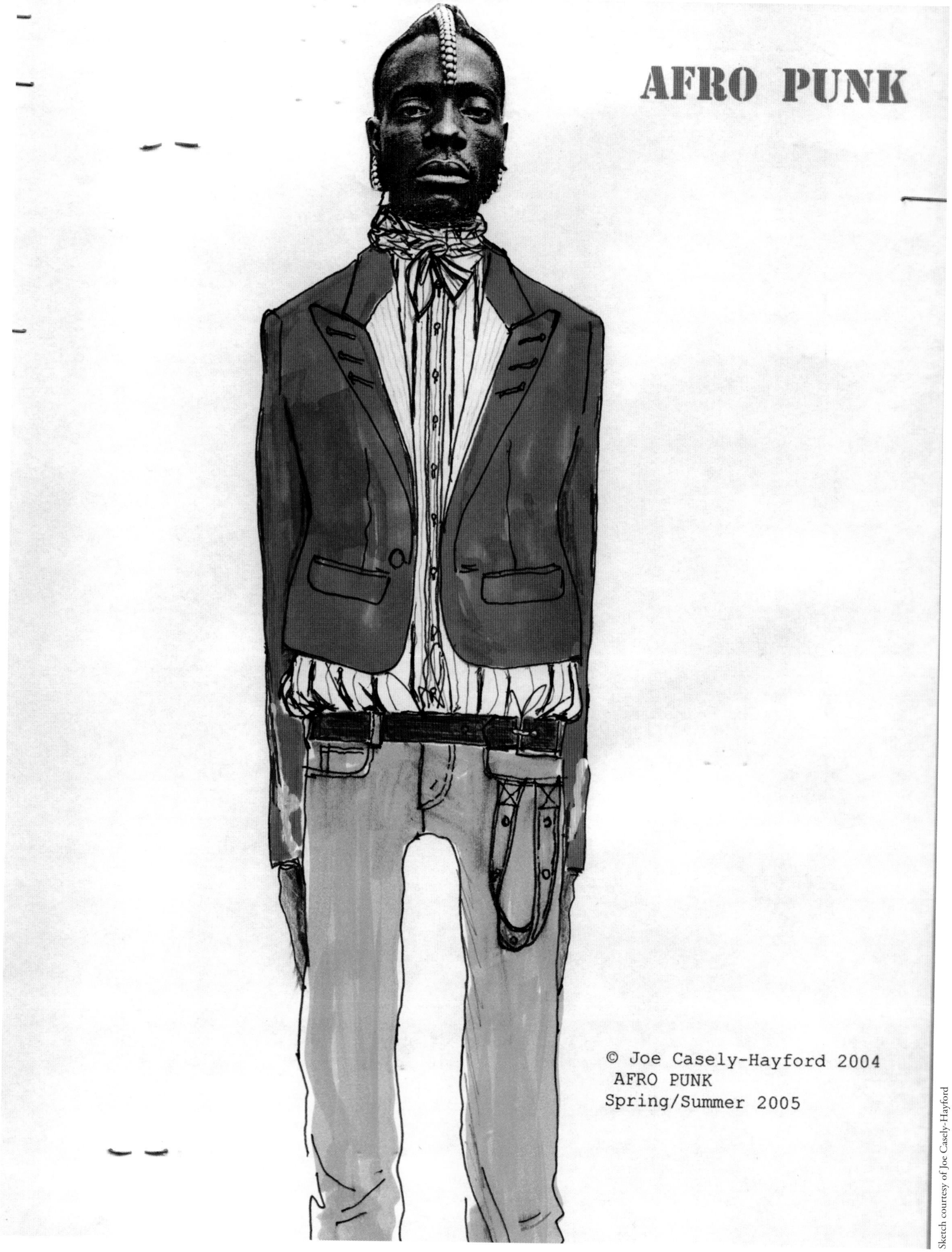

AFRO PUNK

© Joe Casely-Hayford 2004
AFRO PUNK
Spring/Summer 2005

Sketch courtesy of Joe Casely-Hayford

Photography by Gonzalo Fuentes

Jorge Luis Salinas

Latin America is a continent for discovery, especially when it comes to fashion and its relation to culture and folklore: fashion that tends to focus more on international catwalks than its own runways; fashion that induces many Latin American designers to be more receptive to external stimuli than those from within.

This, however, is not the case of Jorge Luis Salinas, whose collections are an example of the extremely rich popular culture of his native Peru. His collections feature the highest quality indigenous fabrics such as alpaca and cotton: boldly interwoven materials and exquisitely delicate embroidery handmade by artisans from different regions of the Andean nation.

Four years of study at the Philadelphia College of Textiles and Science, with a focus on textile techniques and materials, inspired him to take the leap into the world of fashion, free of complexes and inhibitions, in order to show off the best of his native culture and fill fashion runways with color, freshness and coherency. His talent has brought him important awards on national and international runways, such as the Avant-Garde Sport Fashion & Activewear Competition, held in Munich in 1999, and the New Star in Fashion, part of Fashion Week of the Americas 2003.

In a market saturated with industrial products, the work of Jorge Luis Salinas represents a breath of fresh air. There is little doubt that his creations will find a niche for themselves in a world in dire need of the wisdom of traditional craftsmanship.

Photography courtesy of Jorge Luis Salinas

Photography by Gonzalo Fuentes

Hand-sewn dress and sketch of the
dress with fabric samples. From the
2006 collection "Folk," in which the
designer once again showed off mastery
of craft in the form of elaborate,
colorful embroideries.

© Jorge Luis Salinas

- What inspires you?

I was born in a place where the spirit of Incan culture is reflected in myriad rich colors that have endured for centuries. My parents are from the Andes, and this inheritance has enabled me to capture that richness and thereby give form to the material I work with. My goal has always been to recreate and rediscover the exquisiteness of this legacy in a cosmopolitan world, and it continues to be so.

- What is your dream as a designer?

To grow, not just in Peru, but to bring my designs to people everywhere using Peruvian culture as a creative influence.

- What has been the most important achievement of your career?

Returning to Peru. Some time ago, Jill Stuart told me, "You can be a designer anywhere in the world. The only thing you have to do is do it well."

- How important are trends?

The design of innovative fashion produces new concepts of what is and is not beautiful. Trends come and go. You have to know how to take advantage of the moment.

- Fashion has always reflected a certain era. What does fashion reflect in the twenty-first century?

I think it goes without saying that there is an unending struggle to make oneself stand out, to distinguish oneself from the rest. Every great design is a direct response to its time.

- What book would you recommend to every fashion designer?

The street is an open book that we all can read. It offers us thousands of themes, speaks to us about countless people, places and desires. We choose how, when and where to read it.

Jorge Luis Salinas
Industrias Nacionales JL SAC
Calle Pissarro 132, San Borja
Lima, Peru
jorgeluissalinas@terra.com.pe/emporium@emporiumperu.com/www.emporiumperu.com

Photography courtesy of Jorge Luis Salinas

Photography courtesy of Jorge Luis Salinas

Photography courtesy of Jorge Luis Salinas

Photography courtesy of Jorge Luis Salinas

© Jorge Luis Salinas

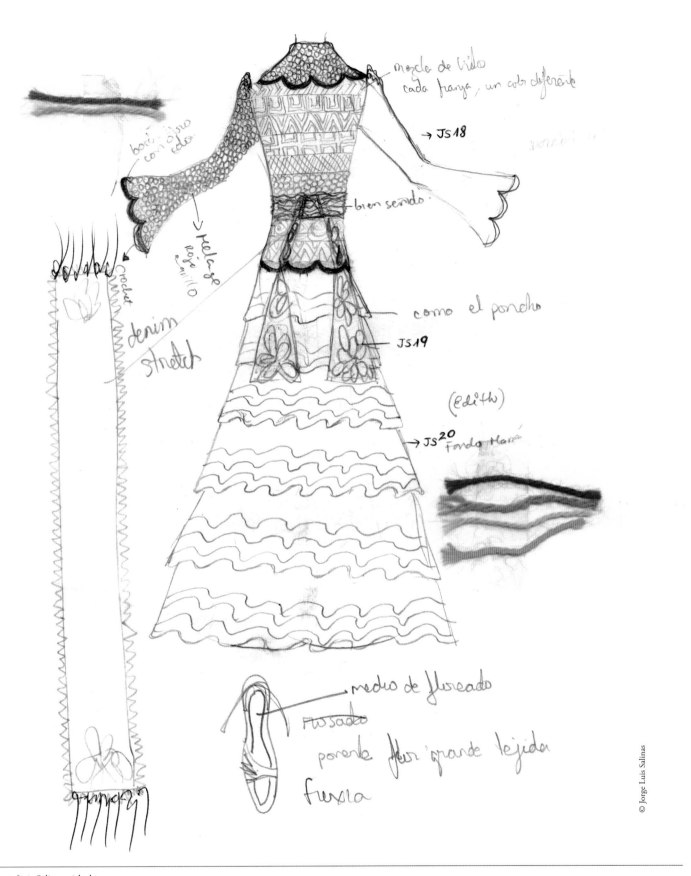

To the left, Jorge Luis Salinas with the design (skirt and sweater) that won him the Avant-Garde Prize at the Gen Art/Nokia Styles International Design Competition. Above, a sketch of the design.

© Jorge Luis Salinas

José Ramón Reyes

Photography by Dan & Corina Lecca

José Ramón Reyes

The decade of the 90s was marked by the indelible print of designers who, fed up with excess, ornamentation and—occasionally—bad 80s taste, felt the need to return to pure lines, sobriety and just the right balance. Helmut Lang and Donna Karan, among others, formed part of this movement which, dubbed "minimalist," has heavily influenced the work of many contemporary designers such as José Ramón Reyes.

Born in the Dominican Republic, a young José Ramón decided to move to New York to study fashion marketing at the Parsons School of Design. At first, nothing suggested that he would abandon a career in marketing and pick up the scissors. In fact, prior to completing his studies, he was already working in public relations for some of the most important press offices in fashion, including those of Helmut Lang and Chanel.

But then something happened that compelled José Ramón to leave his meteoric career in fashion communication and move over to the creative side of the industry: fashion bewitched him. In February 2005, he launched his first collection, characterized from the outset by a taste for quality, simplicity and the combination of "the street" with the most sophisticated and chic, which has become his signature style.

This style, which has resonated deeply among an American public enthusiastic about simple and functional garments, is situated somewhere between pragmatism and one of the main reasons why we dress: to please others as well as ourselves. With the clothing of José Ramón Reyes, achieving this objective is more than assured.

Photography courtesy José Ramón Reyes

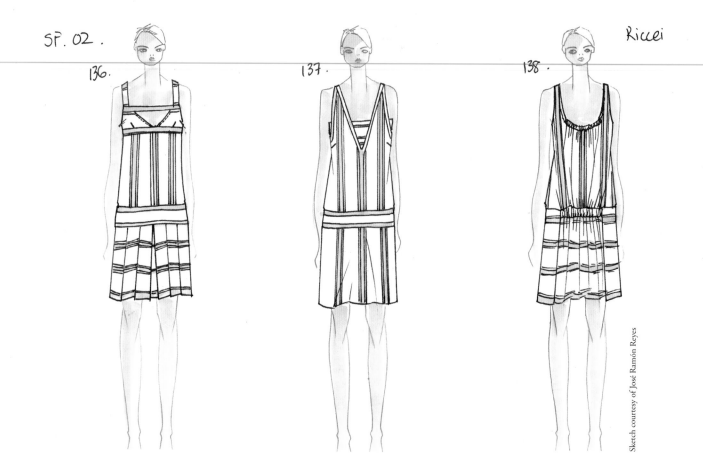

SP. O2 .

136.

137 .

138 .

Ricci

Sketch courtesy of José Ramón Reyes

Above, sketch from the Spring/
Summer 2008 collection. To the right,
a design from the same collection,
which takes inspiration in the casual
fashion of the 20s, with waists at the
hip and knee-length dresses.

Photography by Dan & Corina Lecca

315
José Ramón Reyes

- What inspires you?

Art, music and people on the street.

- What is your dream as a designer?

To be independent and to expand the line into different categories, including accessories and menswear.

- What has been the most important achievement of your career?

To have the courage to start a business of my own.

- How important are trends?

Trends are important for those who follow them. I believe in paying close attention to your instincts.

- Fashion has always reflected a certain era. What does fashion reflect in the twenty-first century?

I think is too early to tell, but what comes to mind is the different choices people have out there. It's not only about the obvious brands, there's an openness in the marketplace for new, young talent. In that respect, I feel very fortunate to live in this century and to be doing what I am doing.

- What book would you recommend to every fashion designer?

Sportswear in Vogue since 1910. It's my second Bible.

José Ramón Reyes

215 West 40th Street, 9th floor

New York, NY 10018

United States

www.reyescollection.com

José Ramón Reyes

Photography by Dan & Corina Lecca

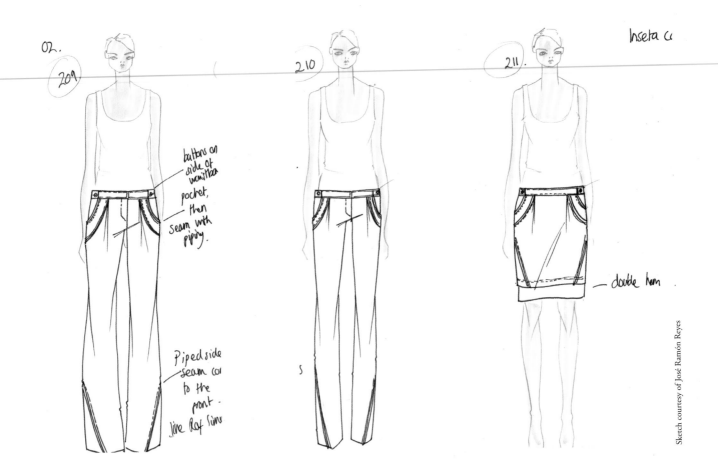

02.

209

210

211

Inseta a

buttons on side of waistban pocket, then seam with piping.

Piped side seam col to the front. like Raf Sims

double hem

Sketch courtesy of José Ramón Reyes

Spring/Summer 2008 collection featuring comfortable garments such as blazers, tweed shorts and wide pants worn at the hip (see image) taken from the male wardrobe and adapted for women, giving the collection that fresh simplicity so characteristic of the work of José Ramón Reyes.

José Ramón Reyes

Photography by Dan & Corina Lecca

JOSEP FONT

Photography courtesy of Josep Font

Josep Font

Raised in the quiet sobriety of a Catalan country house, Josep Font studied architecture and, later, design and pattern design. This diverse training has served him well as a tool in the masterful construction of his own imaginative universe.

His garments have a timeless, elegant, dreamlike quality that transports us to fantasy worlds populated by princesses and fairies, worlds rife with disturbing mysteries. Font's major achievement is usurping the romanticism of the most aesthetically hackneyed places and reinterpreting it in terms of his unique vision. Nothing about him is a cliché. All of his stylistic resources meld to form something new: from winks at Spanish folklore to approximations of the most Parisian chic, not to mention the intense gothic aura peppering the majority of his collections.

Josep's first design success was winning first prize in the Air France contest, held in Paris in 1984. Immediately thereafter, his work appeared in the Clothing Museum of Paris. His work in France is repeatedly the recipient of awards and praise, an exception in the world of Paris fashion and a privilege enjoyed by a select few. In 1989, he was awarded the Fil d'Argent national prize. And in 2008, the Fédération Française de la Couture invited him to take part in Paris Haute Couture Fashion Week. This resulted in his being named the immediate successor of Balenciaga and Pertegaz.

A brilliant career made possible by the hard work of a designer destined to become a legend of Spanish fashion.

Photography courtesy of Josep Font

Sketches courtesy of Josep Font

Above, the planning for the
presentation of the Fall/Winter
2007–2008 collection. To the right,
an empire cut design from this
collection that exudes Josep Font's
trademark austerity.

Photography courtesy of Josep Font

- What inspires you?

Whatever I see or perceive in my everyday life (a movie, a book, a song, a landscape) is susceptible to being transformed into an element that forms part of my collections after being filtered through my own personal interpretation.

- What is your dream as a designer?

A haute couture collection.

- What has been the most important achievement in your career?

I believe that, in life, the best is always yet to come, and the same thing holds true for work. Each new collection is the result of a different process, so it's really impossible to say that one is better than another. In any case, I'd say I got it right the times I came close to achieving some of my objectives after a lot of hard work and effort, such as when I presented my work in Paris. Still, without a doubt, a great deal remains to be done.

- How important are trends?

My work has nothing to do with trends. That is to say, when I set out to create a collection, sometimes I don't have any clear guidelines to follow. Instead, it's a project that takes shape gradually. Since it's a reflection of certain experiences, of a state of mind at a determined moment in time, the result has certain points in common that serve as a thematic thread for the entire collection, but under no circumstances do I allow myself to be carried away by trends.

- Fashion has always reflected a certain era. What does fashion reflect in the twenty-first century?

It's still too soon to say. Check back with me in a few years.

- What book would you recommend to every fashion designer?

History of 20th Century Art.

Josep Font
Ciutat de Granada, 96-98
08018 Barcelona
Spain
www.josepfont.com

Sketches courtesy of Josep Font

Design from the Spring/Summer 2007
collection, presented in Paris under the
title "Princess without a Kingdom" and
dedicated to women who long to be
princesses but whom fate has destined
to a life of struggle.

Photography courtesy of Josep Font

Photography courtesy of Josep Font

Photography courtesy of Josep Font

Images from the Fall/Winter 2007–
2008 haute couture collection
presented in Paris. Embroidery, rich
materials, transparencies, precious
stones: baroque luxury combined with
the monastic serenity in which the
majority of Josep's creations exist.

329
Josep Font

Photography courtesy of Josep Font

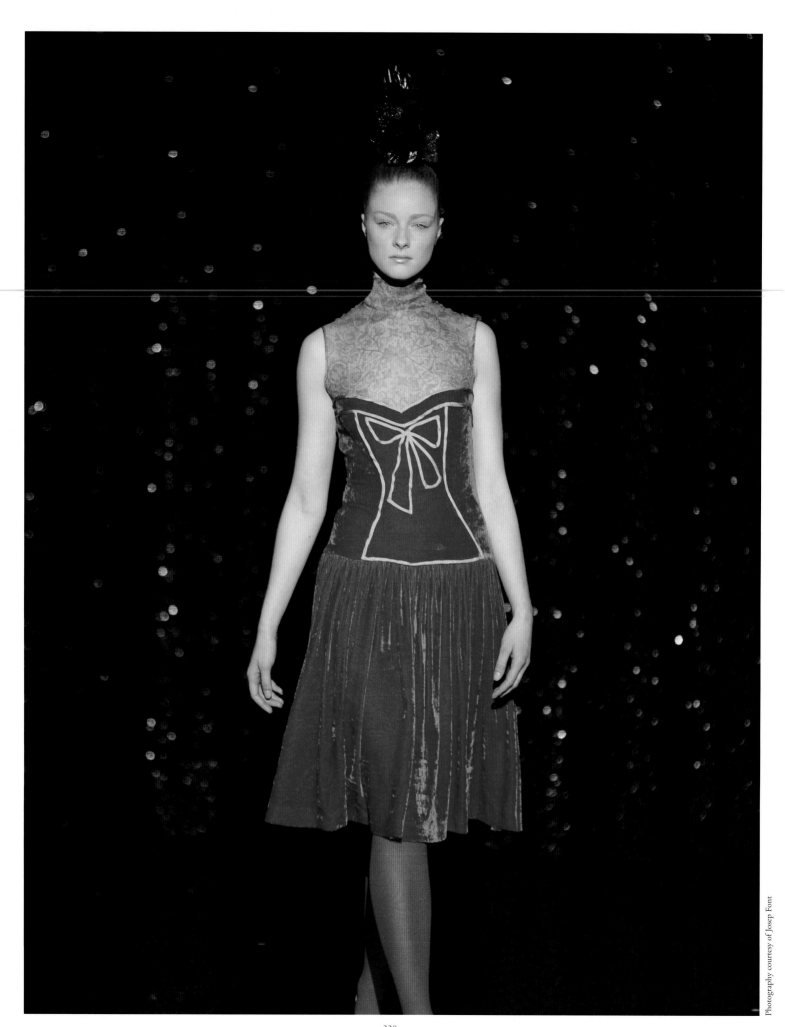

Photography courtesy of Josep Font

Photography courtesy of Josep Font

Two of the designs from the Fall/
Winter 2006–2007 collection with
which Josep Font made his debut on
the Parisian runway, where he revived
the spirit of *Carmen* by turning away
from clichés and demonstrating what
he knows best: dressmaking.

Photography by Simon Lekias

Josh Goot

Josh Goot

Josh Goot not only knows what urban women want to wear in the spring and fall, but also in winter, summer and even the year to come. This Australian designer possesses a nigh telepathic ability for intuiting what the most sought-after skirt in New York is or just what jacket is required to achieve a casual and distinguished, an urban and comfortable look, hence his being dubbed the "king of urban chic."

Josh studied multimedia art and production at Polytechnic University in Sydney. Perhaps his knowledge of media and communications has something to do with his talent for designing clothes for all audiences that are, nonetheless, sophisticated and unique, granting the women who wear them absolute prominence.

His career has been meteoric and fruitful, season after season launching himself as a consolidated force within Australian fashion, a source of pride for this magnificent designer who knows how to make use of his roots in the development of singular garments. For example, his collaboration with Australian Wool Innovation, which Goot assisted in the area of textile research, developing new materials based on merino wool.

Since the presentation of his first collection during New York Fashion Week in September 2006, Josh has known only success and acclaim from New Yorkers smitten by his style. Pure urban chic.

Photography by David Perez Shadi

Josh Goot

© First View

The Spring/Summer 2006 collection of
Josh Goot is like a breath of fresh air on
a hot summer day, where cool colors,
such as blue, exist alongside warmer
ones, such as yellow, all marked by his
signature style, somewhere between
casual elegance and sport.

© First View

- What inspires you?

Life. My travels and experiences. Nature and the big city.

- What is your dream as a designer?

To evolve the aesthetic I love. To make the clothes I believe in.

- What has been the most important achievement of your career?

Moving forward day by day. Being honest.

- How important are trends?

Everything and nothing.

- Fashion has always reflected a certain era. What does fashion reflect in the twenty-first century?

It's fast.

Josh Goot
40-46 McEvoy Street
Waterloo, NSW 2017
Australia
www.joshgoot.com

© Getty Images

337
Josh Goot

Artwork by Shane Sakkeus

Shane Sakkeus was responsible for the
prints in the Spring/Summer 2008
collection, inspired by the different
tones of the sky. With materials
such as silk and georgette, Josh Goot
granted them movement, as if they
were flying among the clouds.

Josh Goot

© Getty Images

Photography courtesy of Simm

Julia y Renata

The fashion universe is built upon common foundations that seek to impose order on the chaos of influences, trends and collections. For this reason, one of the most common ways of talking about non-American and non-European designers is by making reference to the combination of the indigenous and the cosmopolitan. Local identity alongside global identity. Within this play of dichotomies, what is native appears to be wed to tradition, while what is foreign suggests innovation. Nevertheless, this description falls short when it comes to Julia y Renata, because if anything sets these two Mexican designers apart, it's the courage to reinvent Mexican identity beyond all clichés.

Sisters, Julia y Renata live and work in Guadalajara, where they both studied at the Center for Fashion Design. They launched their first line in 1993, and since then have not stopped producing and selling their creations in Mexico City, Guadalajara, Los Angeles and New York.

Julia y Renata are courageous designers, daring to define themselves as Mexicans in a previously compartmentalized universe. Their work has earned them various prizes and acknowledgments with powerful, innovative designs that clearly suggest a willingness to explore beyond the frontiers of convention. They have been selected by *Harper's Bazaar* as being among the most outstanding designers in Mexico, and *Deep* has named them among the thirty-three best and most brilliant Mexicans. This is because Julia y Renata turn conventional taste—along with its atrophied expectations—on its head, doing justice to those who hope that fashion can be genuinely innovative through the variety of creations produced across the globe.

Photography by Esqueda

Photography by Mark Powell

Julia y Renata are the most avant-garde designers in Mexican fashion, always offering experimental creations that explore in depth all the possibilities of design. On both pages, designs from their Spring/Summer 2007 collection.

Photography by Mark Powell

- What inspires you?

Days, situations and people.

- What is your dream as a designer?

To never run out of ideas.

- What has been the most important achievement of your career?

Working together.

- How important are trends?

For us, they serve as a reference for what's happening in the world, but they don't determine the character of our collections.

- Fashion has always reflected a certain era. What does fashion reflect in the 21st century?

A free, heterogeneous, open culture.

- What book would you recommend to every fashion designer?

Any book with inspiring images, ones you can see with your eyes or create with your imagination. We prefer recommending recipes and an album, though.

Julia y Renata

López Cotilla 2061-3 Arcos Vallarta

Guadalajara

Mexico

juliayrenata@yahoo.com

Sketch courtesy of Julia y Renata

Photography by Aiko Kodama

Kanya Miki

In his student days at the Royal Academy in Antwerp, Kanya Miki was already demonstrating his immense talent. It's no surprise, then, that designer Walter Van Beirendonck, a professor in—and now director of—the Fashion Department at the Royal Academy, choose him in 2003 to be his design assistant, a post which, one year later, Kanya took up with British designer John Galliano. In 2005, he decided to found his own label, Kosmetique Label, and present his first collection in Paris.

Having been born in Japan and having studied in Paris, grants Kanya a very personal vision of fashion, one characterized by the unification of the best each culture has to offer. On the one hand, there is the originality and ease for capturing the latest trends and knowing what the street wants—so much a part of Japanese youth culture—while, on the other hand, there is the indisputable value of French fashion, with its ideas about tailoring and durability. What appears to be a dichotomy of principles however, is masterfully overcome in the hands of this gifted young designer.

Moreover, Kanya has accomplished something quite rare: making garments with their own identity, with a trade name, creating a personal cut very much in line with current aesthetics, an idea of beauty that borders on the androgynous, on the frontier between the sexes, granting his creations a decidedly ambiguous character. Indeed, one of his goals is to create a completely unisex line, thereby transcending the limits that clothes have always drawn between the sexes. And there is little doubt that he will pull it off.

Photography by Shun Okubo

Sketches courtesy of Kanya Miki

Both these sketches and this design from
the Fall/Winter 2008–2009 collection
reflect the sobriety characteristic of
both Japanese Comme des Garçons and
Yamamoto, references which Kanya
Miki successfully sifts through in the
formation of his own identity.

Kanya Miki

Photography by Aiko Kodama

- What inspires you?

People or things around me, whatever is happening in reality.

- What is your dream as a designer?

To pursue the creation of both imaginative creativity and reality.

- What has been the most important achievement of your career?

Not yet.

- How important are trends?

A trend is always a reflection from our real life, like a social movement, the economy, the world situation, and so on. It is important for designers to see how the world is moving now.

- Fashion has always reflected a certain era. What does fashion reflect in the twenty-first century?

In the twenty-first century, identity will be more important, so style will be more diversified and complicated. The new sense of luxury must be necessary. It doesn't have to be expensive, but it should be more precious for each individual.

Kanya Miki

16-18, rue Berger

75001 Paris

France

www.kosmetiquelabel.com

Sketches courtesy of Kanya Miki

Sketch courtesy of Kanya Miki

Photography by Aiko Kodama

Sketch and a design from the Fall/
Winter 2008–2009 collection in which
the designer demonstrates several of
his signature characteristics: comfort, a
certain tendency toward oversize and a
taste for apparent simplicity that holds
numerous surprises.

Photography by Derek Henderson

Karen Walker

The collections of Karen Walker take narrative as a source of inspiration. The New Zealand designer delves deeply into different forms of narration, be it through literature, film or theater, in order to represent a woman free of clichés, one who is spontaneous and natural—someone like Woody Allen's Annie Hall, who is capable of combining simple yet original clothes naturally, with a sense of humor and a certain air of insouciance as her signature style. A posture that reveals a certain attitude toward life. The triumph of rebelliousness achieved through work and self-assuredness. A reflection of the training and personality of the designer herself.

Karen began to study pattern cutting and dressmaking when she was only eighteen. Soon she was designing her own shirts, which in three short years would lead to the opening of her own store. And from there the road led straight to success. Karen's designs are sold internationally in 140 stores, in cities such as New York, London, Hong Kong, and Sydney. The most important magazines in the world of fashion devoutly cover her shows. Numerous artists—among them Björk, Sienna Miller, Jennifer Lopez, Claire Danes, Cate Blanchett and Liv Tyler—wear her garments. And not only clothes: Karen has also thrown herself with gusto into the design of jewelry and accessories—all an extension of her unusual know-how.

This is because Karen's sartorial creations are not merely pretty clothes, but garments with an unmistakable identity: a unique, individual personality, one carefully crafted and possible only as the result of the clear-headedness and refined tastes of someone absolutely sure of who she is.

Photography by Derek Henderson

Sketches and images from the Fall/
Winter 2007–2008 collection, "Karen
to the Rescue," in which Karen Walker
introduces us to super-heroines situated
somewhere between the rationalist
sophistication of the 30s and the chic
functionalism of the new millennium.

Sketches courtesy of Karen Walker

Photographies by Corinna Lecca

357
Karen Walker

- What inspires you?

Extremes being pushed together.

- What is your dream as a designer?

To make good product.

- What has been the most important achievement of your career?

There have been hundreds of important moments, and it's impossible to pick just one, but I always feel extremely proud when I see people on the street wearing my clothes.

- How important are trends?

Trends are very important, because they interpret all the thousands of things that are going on on the catwalk into bite-size pieces of information, so the public can get an understanding of what's new in fashion.

- Fashion has always reflected a certain era. What does fashion reflect in the twenty-first century?

Fashion has always reflected shifts in society, and the biggest shift so far this century is our focus on the health of the planet. So, seven years into the century, twenty-first century fashion is about quality, sustainability and functionality to counteract the built-in disposability of fashion and to react to the impact fashion has on the environment. So, in a nutshell, fashion is reflecting our concern for the planet.

- What book would you recommend to every fashion designer?

Anything that has beauty and disaster in the same space qualifies as a fashion icon. For me, one of the books that captures this most is Leo Tolstoy's *Anna Karenina*.

Karen Walker

PO Box 6694, Wellesley Street

Auckland

New Zealand

www.karenwalker.com

Karen Walker

Photography by Derek Henderson

Photography by Derek Henderson

As an extension of the brand, Karen has
made a foray into the world of high-end
jewelry, with creations aimed at a young,
modern sophisticated public. In 2005, she
tried her hand at designing glasses. To the
right, designs from the Spring/Summer
2007 collection.

Photography by Derek Henderson

Photography by Derek Henderson

Photography by Derek Henderson

Ever since she launched her first
eyewear collection, Walker has been
a nonstop success. Her designs,
like those in these images from the
Spring/Summer 2006 collection, are
the favorites of the most die-hard
fashionistas.

Photography by Derek Henderson

© Chanel/photography by Karl Lagerfeld

364
Karl Lagerfeld (Chanel)

Karl Lagerfeld (Chanel)

The contemporary look of Karl Lagerfeld is situated in a classic and cosmopolitan setting. Likely it was this contact with the cultural diversity of Europe that resulted in an identity free of boundaries, one markedly modern and multidisciplinary that leaves its stamp on each one of his creations.

His career began with a sketch of a coat he sent, at the age of seventeen, to a contest held by the Secrétariat International de la Laine, which he won. Balmain then assumed the responsibility of bringing the sketch to fruition and hired Karl to work in their workshop. After that, when he was just twenty years old, he became the artistic director of Patou.

The 60s represented a burst of acceleration in the rhythm of fashion. Pret-a-porter began to establish itself, and Karl commenced a journey as an independent designer throughout Europe, going to work for the Fendi sisters, Chloé, and ultimately launching his own label (Karl Lagerfeld). In 1983, he began a long and passionate relationship with Chanel.

But the designer's restless spirit compelled him to enter other fields. In 1987, he began photographing his own collections, a decision which resulted in genuine works of art. At the same time, he also began collaborating with some of the most prestigious magazines in the world. In 1999, he created a new label—Lagerfeld Gallery—while simultaneously delving deeper into yet another of his great passions, books, starting his own publishing house, Edition 7L. In 2004, this same spirit inspired him to come up with a collection of thirty designs for fashion giant H&M ("Karl Lagerfeld for H&M"). It proved to be a huge success and set a precedent for this kind of collaboration.

© Chanel/photography by Karl Lagerfeld

© Chanel/photography by Karl Lagerfeld

Above, design from the 2006 "Paris–New York" collection. To the right, the sketch *Coco Fitted the 50ties Perfectly*, by Karl Lagerfeld for the French fashion house Chanel.

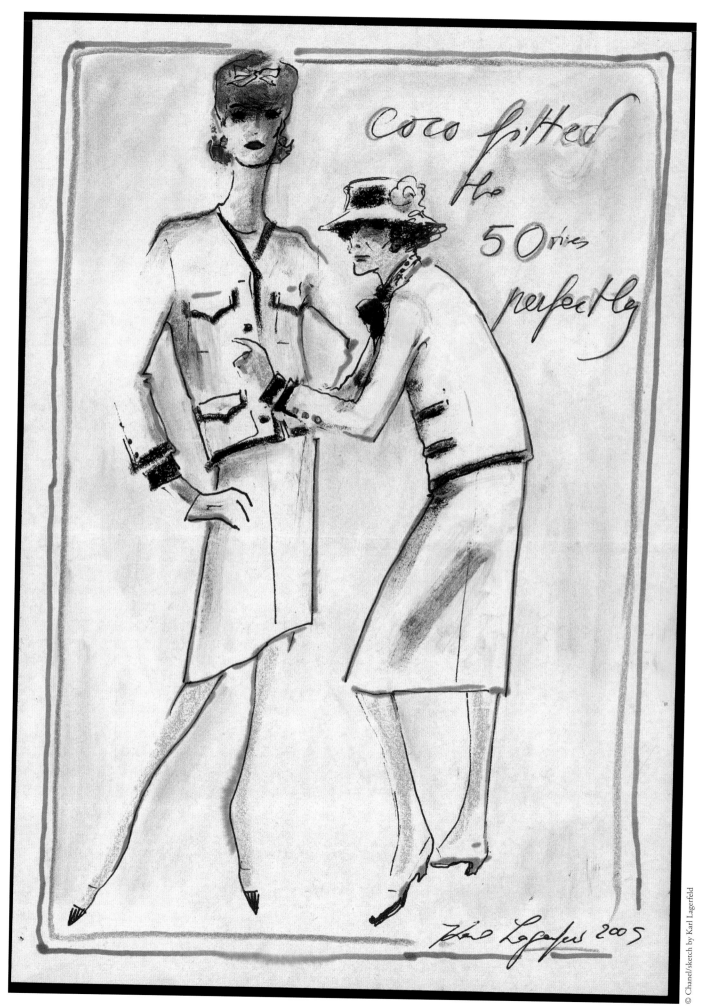

coco fitted
the
50 ries
perfectly

Karl Lagerfeld 2005

© Chanel/sketch by Karl Lagerfeld

- What inspires you?

Inspiration is the opposite of marketing. It mainly comes to me in the morning. When I was a child, I was told, "If you don't get up in the morning, nothing will become of you." Now people laugh at that, but I really get up at seven o'clock, even though I only ever go to bed at two in the morning. There are no rules for inspiration. You have to have your eyes open and like what you see. You have to have a quality view on things, even as you cross the street.

- What is your dream as a designer?

To work in the world of fashion, photography, books; for me, it's sort of like having my childhood dream to be a portrait artist come true, just a little later than expected. Just like design, photography is unique and unrepeatable. In fashion, I don't have an objective audience. I make suggestions, but I don't give out timeless, valid fashion advice. I'm not a moralist. I'm not setting out to improve society through fashion.

- What has been the most important achievement of your career?

My greatest achievement is my next collection. I don't think in terms of success. What pleases me is my job and the way I do it. What's interesting to me is the way of doing the things, not the end. We must reinvent our own destiny.

- How important are trends?

Trends fade away, and I never made a special effort to be trendy. You know, in order to survive, you need to be your own trend. We know how fashion is today, but after tomorrow we don't know.

- Fashion has always reflected a certain era. What does fashion reflect in the twenty-first century?

Today there is a kind of openness. It's very visible, and maybe it's overexposed—me included—but that's funny, too, isn't it? It's funny, because I survived so many people. It's a very strange feeling. But I have no sense of time at all. I'm floating in the air of no time.

- What book would you recommend to every fashion designer?

Grace: Thirty Years of Fashion at Vogue.

Karl Lagerfeld (Chanel)
31, rue Cambon
75008 Paris
France
www.chanel.com

C.C: Are you not tired
of Chanel?
K.L No, only of the
question...

C.C:
So what is your
next crime under
my name?

© Chanel/sketches by Karl Lagerfeld

© All rights reserved

Karl Lagerfeld (Chanel)

© Chanel/photography by Karl Lagerfeld

The photograph to the left, of Coco Chanel with her dog, *Gigot*, was taken in La Pausa, a house owned by the designer on the French Riviera. The image to the right is from the Fall/Winter 2007–2008 haute couture collection.

Karlla Girotto

Photography by Marcio Madeira

Karlla Girotto

When one observes the work of Karlla Girotto, one gets the feeling that she has stored up in her personal chest a large quantity of objects, ideas, fabrics, sensations and mysteries which she turns to at the moment of artistic creation. Like in a child's dream, drawings, forms and sensations merge to give rise to a series of garments charged with feeling and emotion. From this same treasure chest come the materials she uses for her collections, fabrics which, occasionally, are remnants of old garments that she mixes in with new cloth, various objects and anything else that might emerge from her imagination and the sketchbook in which, season after season, she does drawings and gradually develops her collections.

Trained in fashion design at the Faculdade Santa Marcelina in São Paulo, this Brazilian designer of Italian origin burst onto the fashion scene in her country, challenging the increasingly vague limits between art and fashion. In her first shows on São Paulo's House of Designers runway for young talents, she already stood out for her highly personal understanding of the juncture of these increasingly similar universes, which led to the presentation of her work in various art galleries in the most important Brazilian capitals.

After presenting various collections during Fashion Rio, the designer has turned her attention toward the increasingly important São Paulo Fashion Week, where her work has been greeted with much fanfare and critical acclaim. Additionally, she has been able to further develop her multidisciplinary spirit in the form of intense collaborations on artistic projects that lie outside the realm of fashion but run on a parallel course to it, such as her creative forays into dance and theater.

Photography courtesy of Karlla Girotto

Sketch courtesy of Karlla Girotto

Sketch and image from the "Singular" collection. This multi-faceted Brazilian designer normally presents the majority of her collections in the form of a performance, as can be seen in the image on the right.

Karlla Girotto

Photography by Marcio Madeira

- What inspires you?

My life, friends, writers, movies . . . nothing particular and nothing specially. Everything can make my inspirations. Who knows how the world will be in the next second?

- What is your dream as a designer?

In the right moment of my life, I don't have dreams as a designer. I work a lot and hard to make everything, I think. I leave dreams for nighttime and bed.

- What has been the most important achievement of your career?

I'm from a country where everything is very difficult. For me, too many things represent achievements. For example, I finished university (my family didn't have the money, so I studied for free because I was a good student—I had to go!) and I did many fashion shows and can tell people liked it. In the beginning of my career, I did everything alone: sewing, embroidery, painting the fabrics—everything. These are achievements, but they are also lessons, because this is how I learned so many things.

- How important are trends?

Feeling the world, social movements, and having a dialogue with the subterranean and underground layers of society is more important than trends.

- Fashion has always reflected a certain era. What does fashion reflect in the twenty-first century?

Invisible, impalpable feelings. This is the twenty-first century for me. Fashion or not, it's my feeling of the world right now.

- What book would you recommend to every fashion designer?

All the books you are able to read!

Karlla Girotto
Rua Picinguaba, 650
034032-000 São Paulo, SP
Brazil
www.karllagirotto.com.br

Photographies by Marcio Madeira

Karlla Girotto

Images from the "Self-Portrait" collection, a clear reflection of the designer's years of work collecting objects, fabrics, prints, forms and volumes that, in combination, result in her beautiful and highly personal collections.

Photography by Maria Antonia Demasi

Karlla Girotto

Photography by Maria Antonia Demasi

© Skye Parrot

Katarzyna Szczotarska

Katarzyna Szczotarska

Polish by birth and English by adoption, Katarzyna Szczotarska is among those artists who have most successfully reinterpreted the London streetwear of the 80s by uniting it with the influence of such charismatic designers as Martin Margiela.

Trained in her native Poland and a graduate of the London College of Fashion, after two years as chief assistant to Martin, she skillfully navigated the intricate byways of fashion, working for ten years between London and Milan. In 2000, with the confidence that came from working side-by-side with one of the most important designers of all time, she founded her own label, Absolut.

Her creations are conceptual, luxurious, exaggeratedly ornamental and, occasionally, angular in construction. The influence of Russian constructivism, combined with a 60s retro air, can be felt in the majority of her collections.

The clothing of Katarzyna Szczotarska has been defined as "intellectual chic," but behind this label is something that resists classification. Her collections are ascetic and elegant, combining distinguished sophistication with a carefree, spontaneous touch. The result is a timeless, everlasting style, a kind of equilibrium of groundbreaking forms and harmony, which makes her designs easy to wear without having to sacrifice style and good taste.

All of this has made her the deserving winner of the New Generation Award on two occasions, as well as one of the most intriguing designers on the current fashion scene.

Photography by Chris Moore

© Skye Parrot

382
Katarzyna Szczotarska

© Skye Parrot

The common denominator of the
collections Katarzyna is working on
behalf of the modern, sophisticated
super-feminine woman, an objective
toward whose realization the designer
employs all her tools and knowledge.

- What inspires you?

All kind of art, forms, volumes, playing with proportions and ambiguity. I am searching for an emotional response to a garment, an overall impression to like or dislike through a detail invisible to a novice eye and which distinguishes one piece from another. Colors and fabrics inspire me, as well, as they have that amazing power to reinforce and magnify, to go with an idea or to tone it down.

- What is your dream as a designer?

To create a collection or a piece that reflects my vision and aesthetic in timeless perfection. The pretension to intellectualize, to think about concepts too much, for designers and consumers alike, does not attract me. I've got this really natural, almost organic way of creating, and my dream is to provoke a similar passion and response from the public.

- What has been the most important achievement of your career?

The most valuable achievement of my career is the continuous and gradual development of my design skills and my ability to create and give body to my ideas. I am growing a bit more as a designer with every collection, and that is a wonderful feeling. For me, an achievement doesn't mean the end of something; it is just a step toward the next one.

- How important are trends?

Trends come from designers and society. I, therefore, don't follow trends. I create my own interpretations, my understanding of a bigger picture, in a natural and coherent way for me.

- Fashion has always reflected a certain era. What does fashion reflect in the twenty-first century?

Diversity. We don't see unanimous trends like we did in the last century. Designers were more sensitive to political issues in the 60s and 70s, but nowadays it is more about ethical issues, about the designer's conscience, what touches him and what can be done to improve or reduce certain inequalities, like child labor, for example.

Katarzyna Szczotarska
1 St. Stephen's Terrace
London SW8 IDJ
United Kingdom
www.katarzynaszczotarska.com

© Skye Parrot

385
Katarzyna Szczotarska

Sketch courtesy of Katarzyna Szczotarska

Katarzyna Szczotarska

Autumn/Winter 2007

KATARZYNA
SZCZOTARSKA

1

2

3

4

5

Sketch courtesy of Katarzyna Szczotarska

Sketches from the Fall/Winter
2007–2008 collection in which the
Polish designer explores the image of
a contemporary woman interested in
comfort, sensuality and innovation
without abandoning the classical cuts
that suit her so well.

Photography by Chris Moore

388
Kim Jones

Kim Jones

After studying illustration in Brighton and Camberwell, Kim Jones decided to take a different direction in life and applied for a master's program in menswear at London's Central Saint Martins College. To his surprise, he was accepted, despite having no experience whatsoever in the world of fashion. But Kim Jones was already causing a stir and, after graduating in 2003, he presented his first collection at London Fashion Week. Five years later, he won the Menswear Designer of the Year Prize awarded by the British Fashion Council.

Coming from a field other than that of fashion, and having worked as a designer and art director for such avant garde magazines as *Dazed & Confused*, *T: The New York Times Style Magazine*, *Another Magazine*, *10 Men*, *V Man* and *i-D*, Kim has a very progressive vision of fashion, one closely connected to the street. This, along with his impeccable tailoring, has resulted in numerous collaborations as a designer with such labels Umbro (Umbro by Kim Jones), Mulberry, Louis Vuitton, Hugo Boss and the classic Alfred Dunhill.

His Winter 2005 collection represented a perfect fusion of traditional work uniforms and streetwear styles: a clear example of the eclectic vision for which he is famous.

Photography courtesy of Kim Jones

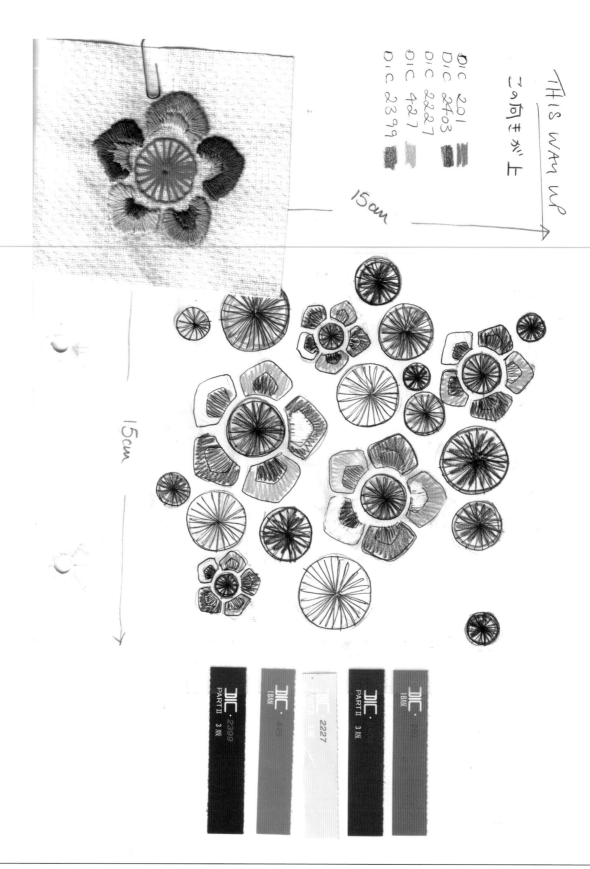

DIC 201
DIC 2403
DIC 2227
DIC 427
DIC 2399

この向きが上

THIS WAY UP

15cm

15cm

DIC • 2399
PART II
3 版

DIC • 427
18 版

2227

DIC
PART II
3 版

DIC
18 版

Above, sketch of the vest worn by the
model in the image on the right, from
the Fall/Winter 2006–2007 collection
entitled "Pop Around the Clock"
featuring designs with a casual cut.

Sketch courtesy of Kim Jones

Photography by Chris Moore

391
Kim Jones

- What inspires you?

I find everything inspires me, mainly music, people, travel and photography. I don't think it's hard to get inspired!

- What is your dream as a designer?

To just be able to get on with what I do and work with the people who I love and get inspired by, whether it's my team, friends, photographers or models.

- What has been the most important achievement of your career?

Still being here, I guess!

- How important are trends?

I don't really think about trends; I just do what I feel. Trends seem to be led by journalists, not designers.

- Fashion has always reflected a certain era. What does fashion reflect in the twenty-first century?

Well, we strive to be modern and, whether that captures the time now or not, it isn't a reflection on the past. Look at the past, but move forward as fast as possible!

- What book would you recommend to every fashion designer?

The one I did with Luke Smalley or Alasdair McLellan, of course!

Kim Jones
www.kimjones.com

393
Kim Jones

Photography by Chris Moore

Photography by Chris Moore

More images from the Fall/Winter
2006–2007 collection, in which
the British designer reinterprets the
classical men's wardrobe, as in this
traditional gray sweatshirt or typical
checked shirt.

Photography by Chris Moore

Kostas Murkudis

Photography by Lars Knorrn

Kostas Murkudis

As a child, Kostas Murkudis emigrated to the German Democratic Republic, where he grew up at a complete remove from the massive bombardment of Western images. These origins, marked by aesthetic sobriety, endowed him with an essentialist, controlled, delicate sensibility, an austere and elegant spirit. His training as an artist began in the prestigious Lette-Verein design school in Berlin. It is no accident, then, that the legacy of the Bauhaus movement can be felt in his work, in the form of a revived functionalism and an objective, rational design that bear witness to the heat of naked flesh, producing a disturbingly sexy effect.

Kostas did not escape the notice of German designer Wolfgang Joop, with whom he worked until the mid-80s. It was at this time that he and Helmut Lang entered into a relationship characterized by a kind of mutual recognition in which they shared work and influences for years. Later, he was tapped by Renzo Rosso to be creative director of New York Industrie. From then on, projects began to multiply: three years cooperating on various interior design collections with designer Kathleen Waibel, leading to the formation of Haltbar Murkudis, through which Kostas's functionalist, comfortable and warm spirit infuses a line of designs for the timeless, cozy home. At the same time, his lingerie designs for the German brand Schiesser represent an exercise in simplicity, functionality and comfort.

All his work is executed with the skill of an artist who knows how to create designs from one piece, and it is this magical fusion of form and content that makes Kostas a master of the essential.

Photography by Jork Weismann

Photography by Jork Weismann

Images from the collection of Kostas
Murkudis for the label New York
Industrie, which sought out the
designer's services to give the brand a
makeover and launch it into the future
through his innovative vision.

Photography by Jork Weismann

- What inspires you?

Everything from people down to virtual travels, movies and traditional craftsmanship.

- What is your dream as a designer?

To see the garments becoming their favorite garment, like a second skin—more and more beautiful after a long distance of time and trends.

- What has been the most important achievement in your career?

Not achieved yet.

- How important are trends?

Don't care about trends at all. When we are talking about trends, we are talking about the description of the already existing. This is not very interesting in terms of research and development.

- Fashion has always reflected a certain era. What reflects twenty-first century fashion?

Ask me the same question in a couple of decades. It is far early to answer this question. There is a certain desire for value.

- The book you would recommend to every designer is…

All the monographies of Rudi Gernreich.

Kostas Murkudis
Bleibtreustrasse 26
10707 Berlin
Germany
www.kostasmurkudis.net

Kostas Murkudis

Photography by Jork Weismann

Kostas Murkudis

Photography by Jork Weismann

Photography by Jork Weismann

To the left, model Guinevere in a
snapshot taken backstage during the
presentation of the Spring/Summer
1998 collection. Above, model Jason in
another image from backstage, though
in this case from the Spring/Summer
2001 collection.

Photography courtesy of Lie Sang Bong

Lie Sang Bong

This acclaimed South Korean designer has no words to describe his work, which is appropriate given that the language he uses does not belong to the realm of words. Lie Sang Bong moves in more imprecise, suggestive waters, using colors, pleats and volumes to create a poetic prose that embraces and encompasses the anatomy of the body. His unusual style synthesizes the elegance French fashion and the exquisiteness of Oriental ways.

With his first collection "The Reincarnation," Bong made a name for himself in Seoul, in 1993. Later, in 1999, he received the Best Designer Prize for his creativity and strong commercial success. In 2002, he made his debut at Paris Fashion Week with "The Timer."

A taste for combination is one of the distinctive features of the work of Bong. The fusion of styles, periods and cultures generates an unmistakably personal manner that this designer-architect cultivates in a natural way.

This is why his shows exude a sense of futuristic women, *femmes fatales* and cuts inspired by Bauhaus principles. Moreover, it is also apparent that the artist, as a result of personalizing all trends and making them his own, has constructed an allegorical language, one that has deservedly elevated him to the heights of his trade, placing him among the five most important Asian designers working today.

Photography courtesy of Lie Sang Bong

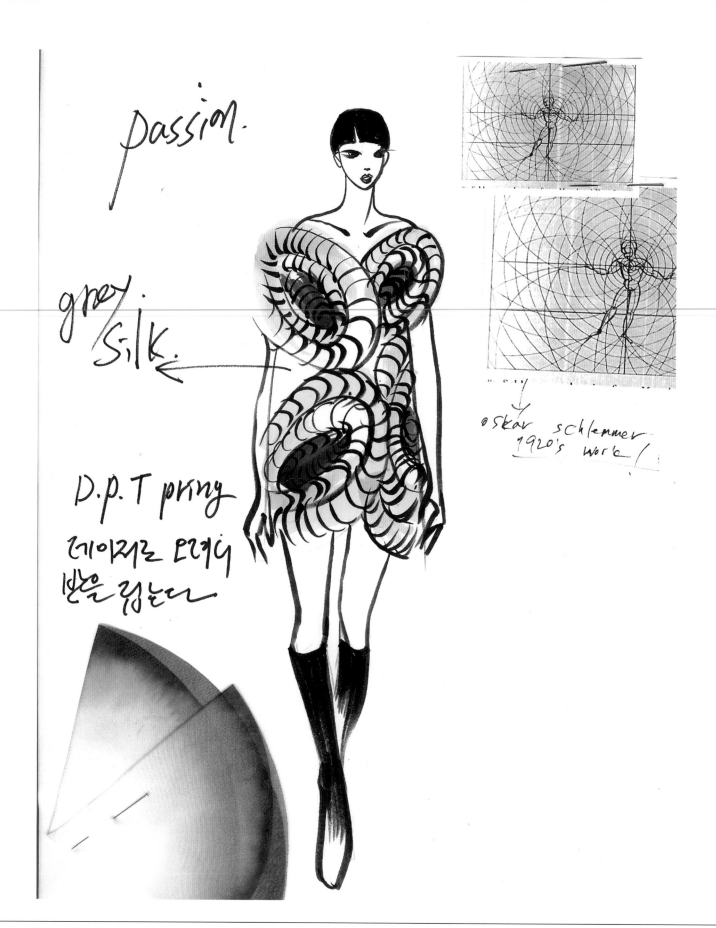

passion.

grey silk.

D.P.T pring
레이져로 프린팅
받은 입는다

oskar schlemmer
1920's work!

Sketch courtesy of Lie Sang Bong

The work of Lie Sang Bong fuses
French elegance and the serenity of
Asian countries. Blended with a species
of poetic futurism, this has made
him one of the most important Asian
designers of late.

Photography courtesy of Lie Sang Bong

- What inspires you?

Anything and everything that surrounds me. Therefore, I play fashion.

- What is your dream as a designer?

To evolve. As I have a philosophy that design is flowing like water; I am dreaming of design which evolves against inertia or else it becomes foul.

- What has been the most important achievement of your career?

It is not my job to name the achievements of my past career. Words don't come easy for me. You, journalists, critics and my customers describe for me.

- How important are trends?

Definitely maybe for other people who think trends are important, yes, possibly maybe. Definitely maybe for people who fully rely on trends, yes, possibly maybe. But they are definitely not for me.

- Fashion has always reflected a certain era. What does fashion reflect in the twenty-first century?

Vorsprung der technik? As fashion is a mirror to the world surrounding it, the biggest difference between twentieth- and twenty-first-century fashion is, I'd dare to say, a "reality TV show." Look at where you are. No longer is the consumer your target market. Now it is the "prosumer." These so-called "reality TV show" phenomena are prominent all over the globe.

- What book would you recommend to every fashion designer?

American Psycho by Bret Easton Ellis, *Der Tod in Venedig* by Thomas Mann, and *The Great Gatsby* by F. Scott Fitzgerald.

Lie Sang Bong

696-26, Yeoksam Dong, Kangnam Gu

Seoul 135-080

South Korea

www.liesangbong.com

Photography courtesy of Lie Sang Bong

pleats를 잡고
hose를 안에
넣는다.

oriental
circle print

Sketch courtesy of Lie Sang Bong

For the Spring/Summer 2008 collection,
the DTP Link Solution printing
method of Yuhan-Kimberly was used.
This allows for the mass production of
unique garments as a way of locating a
middle ground between haute couture
and ready-to-wear.

Photography courtesy of Lie Sang Bong

Sketch courtesy of Lie Sang Bong

Sketch and image from the Spring/
Summer 2008 collection. Guided by
a futuristic vision, the Korean designer
composes original silhouettes, like that
of this yellow dress made with tulle
capes that revolve around the body.

Photography courtesy of Lie Sang Bong

413
Lie Sang Bong

Maison Martin Margiela

Photography by Marina Faust

Maison Martin Margiela

Fashion sometimes follows paradoxical paths, advancing in a kind of zigzag direction as the result of the eruption of contradictory trends, as if with a sudden swerve it sought to leave the beaten path and dart off into uncharted territory, as if with the end of the journey approaching, it decided, suddenly, to change direction and continue further down the road. In this play of continuity and rupture, harmony and questioning, what is constantly brewing is change, evolution. Some follow fashion; others define it.

Among the latter is Martin Margiela. At the core of the firm Maison Martin Margiela is what appears to be a manifesto: the dissolution of the individual within the group—collective work as opposed to the cult of personality. Not even an interview, nor a portrait or a single concession to the star system. The designs of Martin are free of rhetorical elements. His work is characterized by rawness, revealing without artifice the very essence of fashion itself, an aesthetic stance to which this designer continues to be deeply committed.

Born in Belgium and a graduate of the Royal Academy of Fine Arts in Antwerp, Martin worked for five years as a freelance designer and two more for Jean-Paul Gaultier before starting his own company. From the start, his spirit was clearly different. His unstitched, frayed, distorted garments made Martin one of the most important names in fashion in the late 80s and early 90s. For this reason, Martin is an indispensable artist in the world of current fashion. Because mastery of structure is required in order to deconstruct. Because few designers know which thread needs to be pulled in order to strip a garment down to its essentials.

Photography courtesy of Maison Martin Margiela

Photography by Marina Faust

The research carried out by Maison
Martin Margiela is apparent in
"Artisanal": reduced work teams whose
objective is making new garments out
of devalued materials and giving them,
as a result, a new value and a new life.

Photography by Marina Faust

417
Maison Martin Margiela

- How would you describe the relationship between the artistic management and the rest of the team (design department, pattern makers, etc.) and the work system within Maison Martin Margiela?

Our team is quite a soft structure in many ways. Obviously, Martin is the artistic director of the company, and so he works very closely with all the assistants. In a certain way, there is no division between the artistic management and the rest of the team. It is all part of the artistic side for us.

- How many people make up the creative group?

There are seventy-five people at the company. We have another company subsidiary with twenty-five people in Tokyo.

- Given that the designer loses his main character and gives it to Maison's philosophy, is it a "cult of impersonality" that is sought after by Maison Martin Margiela?

No, it is only a matter of switching the importance from an individual to the clothes the designer makes.

- Paris is one of the world's fashion centers. What makes it the most suitable for Maison Martin Margiela?

When Martin ended the Academy in Antwerp, he very much wanted to move to Paris. He wanted to work with Gaultier, which he did for three years. It moves on from there. But we have more than twenty nationalities represented in the company, and you could say many places where the company may exist. Paris is the center of fashion, where people come to buy and so forth . . . it is more a spiritual feeling, but other places would be equally suitable.

- Within Maison's atmosphere, how is it possible to create a trend in fashion? Can this coexist with such a personal product?

Actually, we do not look to create trends in fashion. When you are doing what we do—what Martin does—you are very privileged and very lucky to be in your position. We are just happy to present what we do and to be able to push our boundaries and our limits. It is other people like fashion editors and journalists who create trends in fashion.

- Is the future of fashion to give more significance to the final garment and therefore reduce the designer's personal influences?

We are lucky to celebrate our twentieth anniversary next year. Now people can buy and sell their clothes in many ways, on the Internet, Amazon, e-Bay. We are happy that we have managed to do a little bit of both; making a few pieces and also selling bigger quantities in the shops.

Maison Martin Margiela
163, rue Saint Maur
75011 Paris
France
www.maisonmartinmargiela.com

Photographies by Marina Faust

Photography by Jacques Habbah

In this Spring/Summer 2008
collection, Maison plays with optical
illusions: shirts and undershirts joined
together, pants sewn to jackets, and
scarves that emerge from coat collars,
as in the image on the right.

Photography by Jacques Habbah

421
Maison Martin Margiela

Photography by Giovanni Giannoni

Photography by Giovanni Giannoni

With his Fall/Winter 2008 collection,
made up of astounding volumes and
garments that sheathe the body, Martin
Margiela, as he does every year, proved
why he is one of the most influential
and innovative designers of the last two
decades.

Photography by Ian Guillet

Manish Arora

Born in India and a graduate of New Delhi's National Institute of Fashion Technology, Manish Arora is a designer whose collections skillfully and ironically reflect a term heard with great frequency at the beginning the new millennium: "glocal," that is, the recognition of roots without ignoring the reality of globalization.

Upon completing his studies, he settled in New Delhi, where he soon established himself as a designer and active participant in the world of fashion. In 1994, he won second prize in the Smirnoff Fashion Awards. A year later, he took second prize again in the Young Asian Designers Competition, in which he was also awarded the prize for the Most Original Collection. These awards brought him to the attention of the French edition of *Vogue*, which offered him a job as a designer, an offer which he turned down, preferring to remain in India and continue developing his own label—Manish Arora—and, later, a more informal line: Fish Fry.

In September 2005, he debuted at London Fashion Week. The critical reception was excellent and served as a calling card for Europe and the beginning of collaborations with such big-name brands as Swatch, Reebok and MAC.

And the fact is, the time has come for traditional runways in Milan, Paris and London to be "corrupted" by a rich infusion of designs that break aesthetic molds fixed by the West and make the most illustrious fashionistas squirm in their front-row seats.

Photography courtesy of Manish Arora

Photography by Ian Guillet

Both designs belong to the Spring/
Summer 2007 collection. Amidst
a marvelous staging, new horizons
emerge as the result of the intersection
of two universes: Hindu pop culture
and Western pop culture.

Photography by Ian Guillet

- What inspires you?

I am inspired by love, nature, music—all the things that surround me in my daily life. Inspiration can be found in many things. It could be a movie, a book, a song, a painting, or architecture. If you look, you can find inspiration all around you. Living in India inspires me every day. There are so many different cultures, languages, people and crafts within India—each with their own characteristics—that you can't help but be inspired. One thing that inspires me a lot is traveling. I love to travel. It stimulates my senses.

- What is your dream as a designer?

My dream as a designer is to be loved for my creativity and to give positive energy to everybody who wears my designs; and to add a little humor and fun in people's daily lives. I also want to create a great business which, in turn, can employ many skilled craftsmen in order to revive some of the forgotten crafts of weaving, dyeing and embroideries from India.

- What has been the most important achievement of your career?

I don't think I have really achieved anything so far. I think I have a long way to go before I can say I have achieved something. I don't even know if I am really trying to achieve something. I am just enjoying my work and my life, and this in itself is quite an achievement.

- How important are trends?

I like the idea of trends, but I also believe in the individual personalities that come out in people who don't necessarily follow trends but create their own sense of style. I try not to follow any trends but to create individualistic designs that can be worn over a period of time and can be passed on from one generation to the next.

- Fashion has always reflected a certain era. What does fashion reflect in the twenty-first century?

Twenty-first-century fashion is comfortable to wear, yet it has very strong design elements, very high design mixed with high-quality street wear. It is definitely not very easy to define a certain kind of fashion in the twenty-first century, as so many different designers are creating great fashion, and the consumer has so many amazing choices. I think the twenty-first century is very special for fashion, as many different cultures are influencing global fashion.

- What book would you recommend to every fashion designer?

Memoirs of a Geisha. It really explains how intricately the kimonos were woven in the olden days in Japan and how beautifully they were worn.

Manish Arora
29-35 Rathbone Street
London W1T 1NJ
United Kingdom
www.manisharora.ws

Photographies by Ian Guillet

Photography by Ian Guillet

Photography by Ian Guillet

An exuberant naturalness, full of color
and optimism, is evidenced by many of
the designer's creations, such as these
two designs from the Spring/Summer
2007–2008 collection, which proved a
big hit at London Fashion Week.

Photography courtesy of Zero + María Cornejo

María Cornejo

If you ask María Cornejo about her new collection, she is likely to use words such as "organic," "inspired by nature," and "simple" to describe it, but one could also say that her work is sophisticated, geometric, and utterly urban. This apparent contradiction embodies the essence of her work: a field of forces fueled by the tension between opposites—dark and bright, masculine and feminine, organic and urban. A play of light and shade between which this designer moves with great mastery.

Born in Chile, María moved to England with her family as a young girl. She attended the Ravensbourne School of Art in London, graduating in 1984. Her precocious career took off at once. Before graduating, she was already designing for Fiorucci and the British firm Label. Then she was active in London, Paris, Milan and Tokyo, cofounding the innovative label Richmond Cornejo. Later, she created María Cornejo and worked as the creative advisor for large stores such as Joseph, Tehen and Jigsaw.

In 1996, María and her family moved to New York, where, driven by the deep desire to recover 100 percent control of her work, she transformed an empty space in Nolita. Her artistic evolution has been a process, a work running parallel to her evolution as a person that seems to be pervaded with the emotion she feels from the encounter with nature in the work of her photographer husband Mark Borthwick.

This artistic sagacity led her to be a finalist in 2005 and the winner in 2006 of the Cooper-Hewitt National Design Award, much deserved recognition for an artist who shuns the obvious and reveals what is subtle as a sign of identity.

Photography courtesy of Zero + María Cornejo

Photography by Monica Feudi

Based on simple forms, María
Cornejo's Fall/Winter 2007–2008
collection has a notable organic
component as well as sensual cuts
reminiscent of elements from the
animal and plant worlds such as
chrysalises, leaves and mushrooms.

Photography by Monica Feudi

435
María Cornejo

- What inspires you?

I usually get inspiration from very abstract things and when I am not really looking for it—when it is least expected —like when I touch fabrics and an image instantly pops into my head.

- What is your dream as a designer?

To keep learning, to continue to be inspired and stimulated and never be bored.

- What has been the most important achievement of your career?

I was extremely honored when I was awarded the Cooper-Hewitt Design Award in 2006. To be recognized for innovation by my peers in other fields such as design, architecture, product development and landscape was incredible.

- How important are trends?

I'm not interested in trends. I believe you have to decide what suits you, regardless of fashion and trends (*B-Guided* and *The Independent*).

- Fashion has always reflected a certain era. What does fashion reflect in the twenty-first century?

Sportswear and casual wear have marked the fashion of the twenty-first century.

- What book would you recommend to every fashion designer?

I used to love flipping through this book of indigenous costumes back when I was a design student.

María Cornejo

33 Bleecker Street

New York, NY 10012

United States

www.zeromariacornejo.com

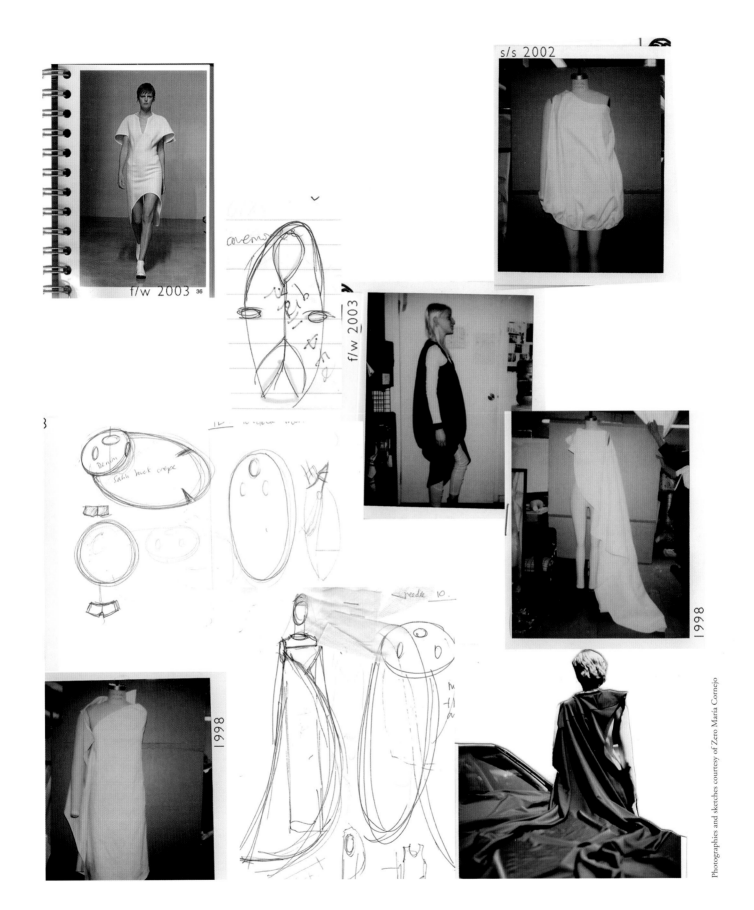

s/s 2002

f/w 2003 36

f/w 2003

1998

1998

Photographies and sketches courtesy of Zero María Cornejo

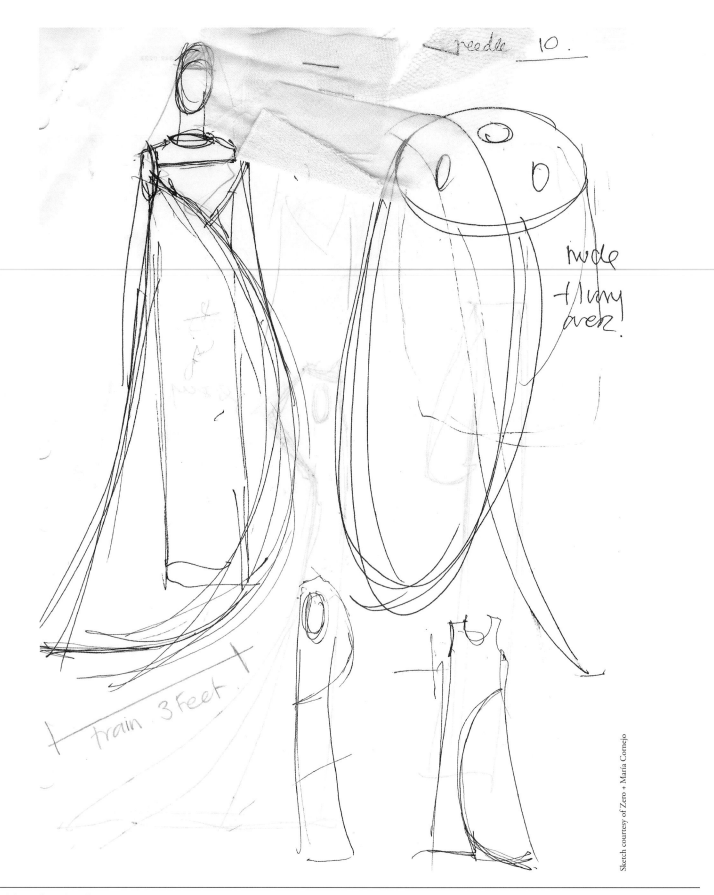

needle 10.

nude turny over.

train 3 feet

Sketch courtesy of Zero + María Cornejo

Sketch and design from the Fall/
Winter 2007–2008 collection,
featuring natural fabrics such as silk,
cashmere and cotton and subtle forms
represented by the voluminous coat
with rounded lines that appears in the
sketch.

Photography by Monica Feudi

439
María Cornejo

Martin Grant

Photography by Frederique Dumoulin @ Java

Martin Grant

No creative form exists in a vacuum, given that the process of creation tends to implicitly involve the need to examine disciplines that converge with or run parallel to the one in which the artist is working. Such is the case of Martin Grant, an Australian designer who, after a brilliant seven-year career in fashion, decided to return to school, enrolling as a sculpture student in the Victorian College of the Arts with the aim of approaching his own field from a distinct perspective.

After completing his studies, he headed for London, where he worked for different companies until, in 1992, he relocated to Paris and dedicated himself to his own fashion label: first in the form of small collections and later opening his first boutique in 1996 in an old barber's shop in the historic Marais district.

Martin has blazed a trail for himself, remaining faithful to a work philosophy characterized by a marked affection for customized tailoring, detail and simplicity of lines. These features are, beyond all doubt, the hallmark of this designer who, in each of his collections, provides us with a lesson in geometry and proportion, in the never-ending search for an eternal beauty so difficult to find.

Alongside his work in fashion, he has also participated in artistic projects which have allowed him to combine his two passions—design and sculpture—such as the year 2000 calendar he created for Absolut.

Photography by Vivien Allender

Sketches courtesy of Martin Grant

Fall/Winter 2007–2008 collection, noteworthy for the meticulous preparation of each of its garment and a taste for detail. Above, sketches by the designer for the collection. To the right, some of the designs.

Photographies by Frederique Dumoulin @ Java

443
Martin Grant

- What inspires you?

Nature, open spaces, old cities, architecture, strong characters, personal interiors, Rome, Venice, India and Paris.

- What is your dream as a designer?

To be able to produce one collection per year instead of six!

- What has been the most important achievement of your career?

To still be existing as a designer.

- How important are trends?

For me, trends are not important, and I try to avoid them at all costs.

- Fashion has always reflected a certain era. What does fashion reflect in the twenty-first century?

The death of fashion as we have known it for the last century.

- The book you would recommend to every fashion designer is...

, by Albert Lamorisse.

Martin Grant

10, rue Charlot

75003 Paris

France

www.martingrantparis.com

Martin Grant

Photography by Frederique Dumoulin @ Java

With this silver-lame mermaid-style
evening gown, the Australian designer
topped off the presentation of his Fall/
Winter 2007–2008 collection.

Photography by Frederique Dumoulin @ Java

Photography by Frederique Dumoulin @ Java

Martin Grant

Photography by Frederique Dumoulin @ Java

Photography by Frederique Dumoulin @ Java

In the Fall/Winter 2007–2008
collection, Martin Grant plays with
a palette of whites, blacks, grays and
purples on structured silhouettes,
occasionally with volume and a touch
of brilliance for the night, as in these
two designs.

Mikio Sakabe

Photography by Daniel Sannwald

Mikio Sakabe

The universe of Mikio Sakabe is a utopia ornamented by the futuristic imaginings of cinema and manga aesthetics. From the expressionism of Fritz Lang to Blade Runner and Brazil. From Russian constructivism with small, baroque Hundertwasserean brush strokes to manga comics. From Western artistic icons to the popular culture of Japanese dolls.

All of this condenses into an ambient nightscape, closed-off, full of neon and tunnels, a space far from nature that builds its lair in technology. A fantastic human species, halfway between human and cybernetic, endowed with the daintiness of geishas and the strength of replicants.

This very young Japanese designer began his career in Paris and Belgium, reaping numerous awards and much praise along the way. Mikio has three stupendous and unique collections to his credit. They are rife with urban references, transporting us to another world through aesthetically complex designs such as the garments in his "20XX" collection, which features an entire city incorporated into the pieces (churches and buildings included), or the simple, utilitarian, pragmatic designs featured in the collection "Industrial Dolls."

Fashion, in a way, always has its foundation in an ideal, a perfect show. To give shape to his vision, Mikio has successfully fused a wide range of cultural influences, all the elements needed to create his personal cosmos. For this reason, he is considered one of the most original figures on the international fashion scene today.

Photography courtesy of Mikio Sakabe

Photographies by Daniel Sannwald

These two images belong to the Spring/ Summer 2008 collection "Industrial Dolls," conceived as way of offering comfortable, functional garments within a very constructivist line.

Sketches courtesy of Mikio Sakabe

- What inspires you?

Everyday life, especially when I'm alone.

- What is your dream as a designer?

To make my image collection complete without any limits.

- What has been the most important achievement of your career?

The moment I found what I want to do is fashion.

- How important are trends?

I don't know trend so much.

- Fashion has always reflected a certain era. What does fashion reflect in the twenty-first century?

Fashion will become minimum, pure and emotional.

- What book would you recommend to every fashion designer?

Every manga.

Mikio Sakabe
4-13-1 Chuo Nakano
Tokyo 163-0011
Japan
www.mikiosakabe.com

Mikio Sakabe

Photography by Daniel Sannwald

Sketch courtesy of Mikio Sakabe

Illustrations by the Japanese designer in
which free rein is given to his personal
universe, one replete with references to
Japanese youth culture, such as these
adolescents in uniforms with cotton
clouds against a backdrop of Little
Twin Stars dolls.

Mikio Sakabe

Sketch courtesy of Mikio Sakabe

The collection "20XX," featuring skyscrapers and buildings printed on the garments, captivated the world of fashion and earned Mikio Sakabe the Mango Fashion Award 2007, presented to him by Valentino.

Photography by Daniel Sannwald

Photographies by Daniel Sannwald

© minä perhonen/photography by Makiko Takehara

minä perhonen

Behind the minä perhonen label is Japanese designer Akira Minagawa, who, in 1995, founded the fashion company minä, which three years later would become what we know today as minä perhonen.

The strong bond that has united this designer for years to Scandinavian culture and art was the origin of the new name. Adopted from the Finnish, *minä* means "I," and *perhonen*, "butterfly," an allusion to the patterns on the insects' wings that occasionally coincide with his own designs.

If anything characterizes minä perhonen, it is the meticulousness and care that go into the design and production of its garments. Akira's designs begin on paper, the result of his careful research of different fabrics and tailoring styles. Traditional methods typical of the locality are employed to bring these designs to fruition. His garments are manufactured either at his own workshop, in the residential area of Shirokanedai in Tokyo, or in small factories on the outskirts of town run by traditional tailoring houses that preserve ancestral tailoring techniques. The fabrics, designs, drawings, illustrations, quality, embroidery and unique wadding methods are the main ingredients that give the minä perhonen label its inimitable personality.

In a world defined by the dislocation of production and fast fashion, the work of Akira represents something new, something removed from the standard production practices of current fashion, creations that resist the passage of time, ones that endure.

Photography by Norio Kidera

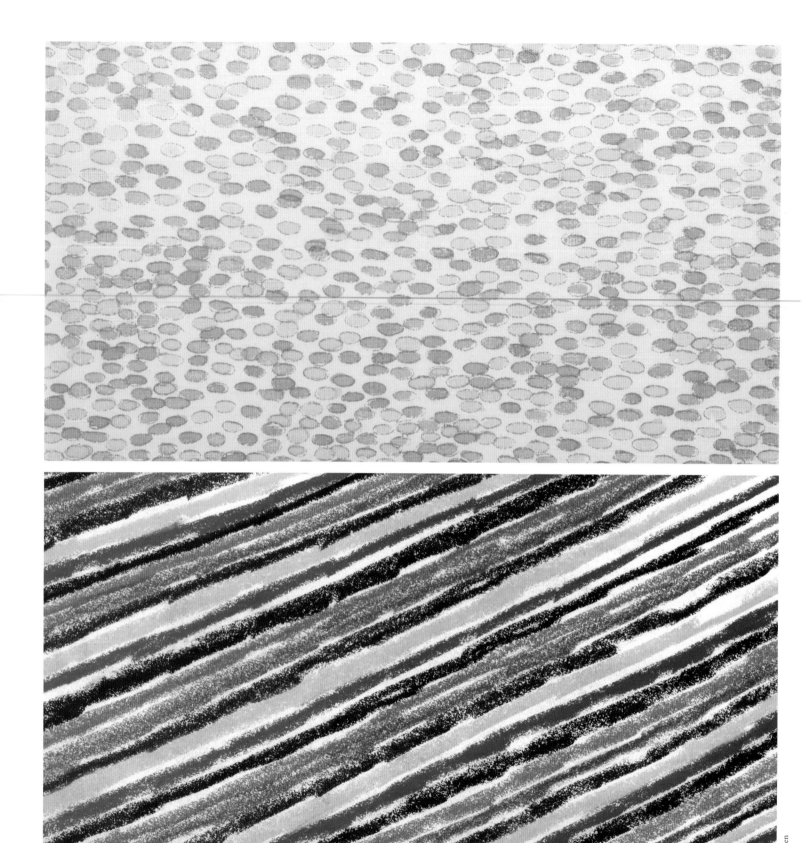

© minä perhonen

Above, two illustrations by minä perhonen: Jellybeans (top), from the Spring/Summer 2002 collection, and Crayonniste (bottom) from the Fall/Winter 2007–2008 collection, which served as the base for the print of the dress on the right.

© minä perhonen/photography by Makiko Takehara

- What inspires you?

I am inspired by all the experiences that take place around me, by all the events in society and in nature that occur in the world.

- What is your dream as a designer?

Indefinite trust between good manufacturers and us, and a quest for imagination.

- What has been the most important achievement of your career?

The simple fact that our creation has been continued for now. It is amazing.

- How important are trends?

I think it is important for each fashion designer to think about the (ideal) way of society, not about trends.

- Fashion has always reflected a certain era. What does fashion reflect in the twenty-first century?

The harmony of the world. It is not the "standardization" but the harmony that is achieved with respect to individual creations. I hope fashion reflects this harmony, like each creation appearing differently in the world.

- What book would you recommend to every fashion designer?

I might not name a book. Each designer would find books for him/herself.

minä perhonen

10F, 5-18-9 Shirokanedai, Minato-ku

Tokyo 108-0071

Japan

www.mina-perhonen.jp

© minä perhonen/photography by Makiko Takehara

© minä perhonen/photographies by Makiko Takehara

Presentation in Paris of the Fall/
Winter 2007–2008 collection, in
which the label minä perhonen offers
its meticulous creations, centered on
prints and elaborate pieces of crochet.

© minä perhonen/photography by Makiko Takehara

Photography courtesy of Neil Barrett

Neil Barrett

Neil Barrett's creations possess a special charisma. His refined, waisted suits fit like a glove, granting the person wearing them a rakishly elegant rebelliousness, a complex equilibrium arrived at thanks to the skillfulness of a designer brimming with talent.

Neil ranks among the most intriguing fashion designers on the current scene. He studied at Central Saint Martins and cut his teeth at some of the best labels in the business. He was first tapped by Gucci to design their men's line, a position he held until 1994. At that time, he began working as the creative director of Prada's men's line.

Neil's connection to this firm translated into a doubling of sales between 1994 and 1995, as well as the certainty, for Neil, that he possessed the requisite talent and charisma to successfully move his firm forward. To that end, Neil presented his own men's collection in 1999, to which, years later, he added the women's collection that he presents every year at Milan Fashion Week. On top of this, the collaboration with Puma and the long waiting list of actors and musicians anxious for Neil to dress them.

It is likely that his success resides in an exact combination of elegant designs and street wear. All of his garments are easy to wear, endowed with a versatility that makes them appropriate for any occasion, with a strong dose of avant-garde added to the mix.

These qualities have made Neil one of the most observed designers of the moment, cultivating his vision one step ahead of fashion trends. And in the world of fashion, this is priceless.

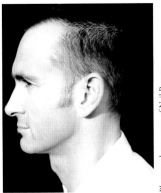

Photography courtesy of Neil Barrett

Sketch courtesy of Neil Barrett

Above, designer specifications for the
shirt worn by the model on the right.
In a sleight of hand, the designer
fashions back pockets and front pleats
on the shirt.

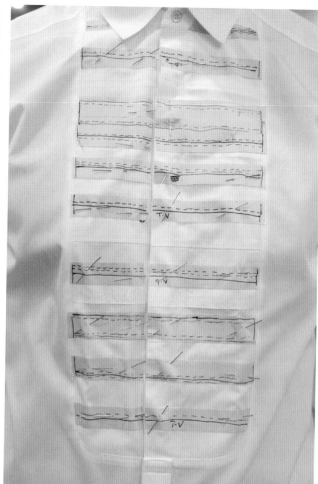
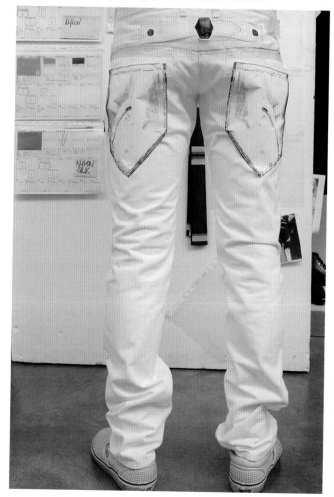
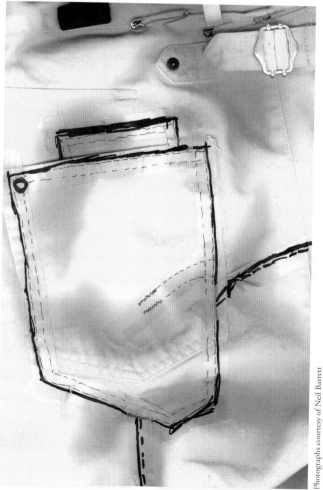

Photographs courtesy of Neil Barrett

- What inspires you?

Inspiration for me comes throughout the day and night, when you specifically look for it or when you least expect it, by allowing your senses to be inspired by any object, situation or mood and then following your first instinct.

- What is your dream as a designer?

To continue to increase the frequency with which I see people for whom I have personal esteem for their talent in their chosen careers, wearing Neil Barrett.

- What has been the most important achievement of your career?

After just eight years since my first collection, hitting 65 million euros worth of retail sales in 2007 has been a milestone for me as an independent designer, without advertising or PR, without a financial or production backer, which shows that people have bought for the clothes' sake and not for a hyped PR brand.

- How important are trends?

I believe in following my instinct. In the end, a trend for me is when you feel strongly for some element of design or styling, and this is picked up by the stylist, journalists or buyers. For this reason, trends are relative. It really depends on individual taste and not a general consensus.

- Fashion has always reflected a certain era. What does fashion reflect in the twenty-first century?

The world is a smaller place today, through media and travel accessibility. Influences from the world over are present in today's wardrobe. I believe it's acknowledging both the past and present and combining them through a futuristic filter that will reflect what is new in this century.

- What book would you recommend to every fashion designer?

Citizens of the Twentieth Century, by August Sander.

Neil Barrett
Via Savona, 97
20144 Milan
Italy
www.neilbarrett.com

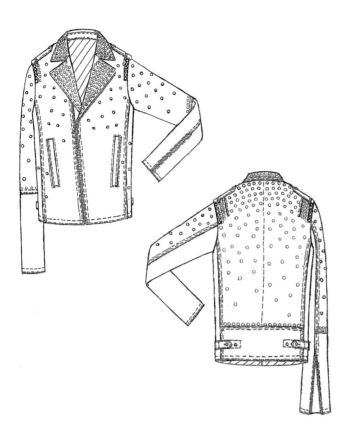

Photographs and sketch courtesy of Neil Barrett

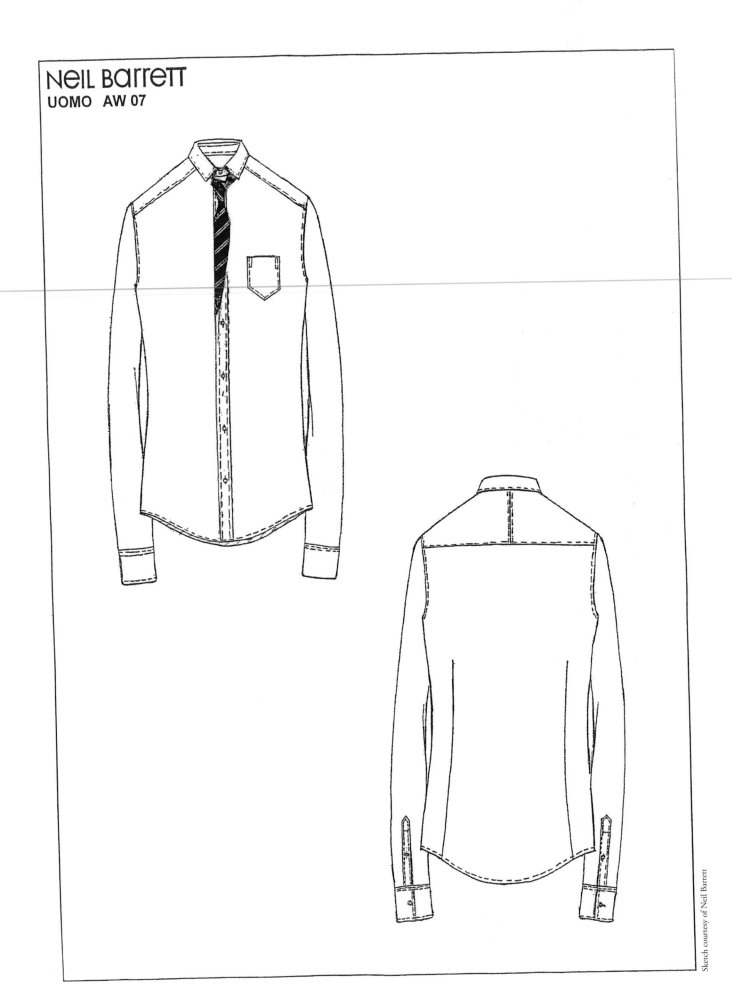

Sketch courtesy of Neil Barrett

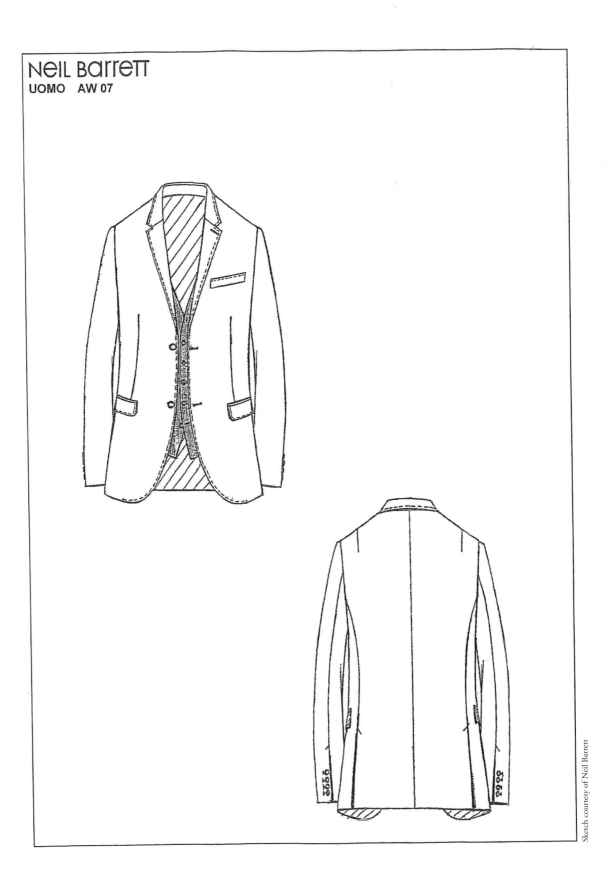

Sketch courtesy of Neil Barrett

Designer specifications for the
Fall/Winter 2007–2008 collection,
consisting of classical garments
interspersed with parkas, immaculate
leather jackets with studs, and
motorcycle boots: the perfect union of
eternal elegance and roguish vitality.

Photography courtesy of Nina Donis

Nina Donis

Born in Moscow, Donis Pouppis spent the bulk of his childhood and adolescence in Cyprus. In 1996, he left the Mediterranean island to attend the Textile Academy of Moscow, where he met the person who would become his fellow traveler, Nina Neretina, an art student from a town close to Voronezh who headed for the Russian capital after graduating from college. From this encounter, an uncommon aesthetic was born, one situated somewhere between the functionalism of Soviet constructivism, avant-garde and continuous references to pop culture.

Nina Donis, the brand created by the two, was gradually making a name for itself, with designs appearing on Russian runways and—sporadically—European ones, before making the definitive leap to London Fashion Week, soon enjoying the recognition and international projection this achievement brings.

Along the way, Nina Donis has collected numerous acknowledgements and awards, including the Mix Collection Prize of the 2001 International Festival of Fashion and Photography, held in Hyères and representing a meeting place for young designers, and the Designer of the Year Prize, awarded by the Russian edition of *Harper's Bazaar*.

The design tandem Nina Donis is a clear example of how the Russian fashion panorama is in full swing, with a wide and varied range of proposals certain to leave no one indifferent.

Photography courtesy of Nina Donis

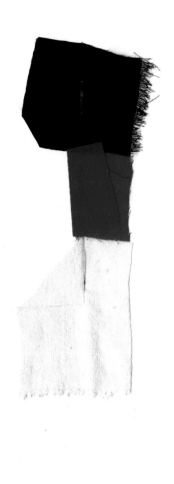

With white and black colors in the background, and reds and oranges as effective combinations, Nina Donis structured her Spring/Summer 2008 collection, from which a sketch and one of the designs have been selected for these pages.

Sketch courtesy of Nina Donis

479
Nina Donis

Photography courtesy of Nina Donis

- What inspires you?

Everything around me, life, recollections and dreams.

- What is your dream as designers?

To have the opportunity to do what we love most of all for as long as possible.

- What has been the most important achievement of your career?

The most important achievement is our long-term cooperation with each other and the delight we are still taking in it.

- How important are trends?

Trends are needed to make fun of them.

- Fashion has always reflected a certain era. What does fashion reflect in the twenty-first century?

Chaos and vanity.

- What book would you recommend to every fashion designer?

Encyclopedia of Arts and *World Art History.*

Nina Donis

Nizhniy Susalniy per., 5 str. 5a.

105064 Moscow

Russia

www.ninadonis.com

Sketch courtesy of Nina Donis

481
Nina Donis

Sketch courtesy of Nina Donis

Nina Donis's profound knowledge
of fabrics and simple style have
transcended Russian borders and
arrived to the catwalks of London
Fashion Week, earning the designers
their various awards on their journey
across the European continent.

Photography courtesy of Nina Donis

483
Nina Donis

Sketch courtesy of Nina Donis

An apparently casual, simple air
and complexity of form, as well
as the strong influence of Russian
constructivism, were the dominant
features of the Spring/Summer 2008
collection of the Moscow duo.

Photography courtesy of Nina Donis

485
Nina Donis

Photography by Paola Kudacki

Pablo Ramírez

"Blessed satin neckline that feigns modesty, in you I trust. Perfumed tenderness of silk, purest line of large pleats, spring-summer, have pity on us." With these words in the form of prayer, a murmur reminiscent of a typical square situated alongside a church, Pablo Ramírez presents his work to us on an unusual webpage. Practically psychoanalytic in nature, his work is most likely an unconscious reflection of his childhood experience of Catholic school in a small town in Argentina.

Nuns, girlfriends, schoolgirls, gauchos and tango lovers form part of the rich and personal imagined world of this Argentinean designer born in Navarro, not far from Buenos Aires. Trained in fashion design in the Argentine capital, Pablo worked for years as a consultant for different casual clothing brands, among them Gloria Vanderbilt, until, in 2000, he decided to debut his own label: Pablo Ramírez. This signaled the beginning of a prolific career, which involves not only the creation of his own collections, but also participation as a designer in numerous ballets operas, films and other artistic projects.

If one word could define the work of Pablo Ramírez, it would be "religion," not simply because of the religious connotations apparent in his creations, but because of his fervent love of fashion, a devotion which has led him to delve courageously and without prejudice deep into his own interior.

Photography by Gabriel Rocca

Sketch courtesy of Pablo Ramírez

Above, illustrations in the form
of silhouettes by the Argentinean
designer. To the right, an image from
the Fall/Winter 2006–2007 collection,
featuring garments full of sobriety,
romanticism, and the color black.

Photography by Gabriel Rocca

489
Pablo Ramírez

- What are inspires you?

What I draw, which I'm always doing, is my main source of inspiration. After that, movies, reading, books in general, history and Buenos Aires.

- What is your dream as a designer?

To be at peace with what I do, enjoying it more and achieving a stable and secure existence.

- What has been the most important achievemente of your career?

Always trusting my instincts and striving never to betray myself.

- How important are trends?

Not very. When trends get too close to my work, I start searching for another way.

- Fashion has always reflected a certain era. What does fashion reflect in the twenty-first century?

Individuality.

- What book would you recommend to every fashion designer?

I don't think I could recommend just one book. There are millions; it depends on the individual.

Pablo Ramírez
Perú 587
San Telmo, Capital Federal
Argentina
www.pabloramirez.com.ar

Pablo Ramírez

Sketch courtesy of Pablo Ramírez

Above, illustrations from the Fall/
Winter 2006–2007 collection. To the
right, designs from this collection (top)
and the 2005 collection (bottom),
which was presented as a performance
in the Museum of Latin American Art
in Buenos Aires.

Sketches courtesy of Pablo Ramírez

Photographies by Gabriel Rocca

Photography by Cecilia Glik

Pablo Ramírez

Sketch courtesy of Pablo Ramírez

Both pages show illustrations by the designer. Markedly naïve in nature, they give representation to the child-like imaginings very much present in all his work.

vestido lana/organza !!

cardigan y
bermuda masc. lana

falda tablas lana

blazercito veranos lana

chaquita lana

falda lana

Laura
Sosa!

Sketch courtesy of Pablo Ramírez

Photography courtesy of Rick Owens/model: Terry Ann

Rick Owens

His creations suggest aesthetic rigor and a certain distinguished yet casual spirituality, a style at odds with the predominate aesthetic of his native city of Los Angeles. The designer has fashioned a personal name for himself to define his style: *Glunge*. That is, a combination of glamour-slash-grunge, the fusion of elegance and insouciance, a refined version of grunge and Belgian deconstrucionism with a certain nostalgic nod to the most classical elegance.

This unusual designer studied painting at Otis Parsons Art Institute in Los Angeles, after which he devoted two years to learning patterning and cutting techniques. He then worked for different California companies before starting his own business in 1994, selling his work to an exclusive Los Angeles retailer by the name of Charles Gallay.

Gradually, he began showing his work to international buyers and accumulating clients. Eventually artists of such stature as Madonna and Courtney Love were outfitting themselves in his creations.

The designs of Rick Owens make up the wardrobe of an unconventional personality, one stripped of ornamentation and consisting of subtle, beautiful, intimate garments that avoid sensational affectation and leave a mark that withstands the test of time.

His achievements turned him into a regular on the New York catwalk until 2003, when his collaboration with the prestigious firm Revillon resulted in his relocating to Paris, a city where he has furthered his design mastery while remaining faithful to a unique style.

Photography courtesy of Rick Owens

Photography courtesy of Rick Owens/model: Ekaterina

The Paris-based California designer toyed with deconstruction, volumes and forms in the creation of these designs, from 2006, charged with a certain air of mystery.

Photography by Dan Lecca

Photography courtesy Rick Owens

- What inspires you?

I always get inspired by modernist architecture and coffee, usually together.

- What is your dream as a designer?

My dream was to find a comfortable corner in which to create freedom. I'm very grateful that I found it.

- What has been the most important achievement of your career?

To have ended up with such an elegant team to work with me.

- How important are trends?

When I'm in one mood, I think of trends as a symbol of good-natured collective consciousness. When I'm in another mood, I see trends as something pleasant to react against.

- Fashion has always reflected a certain era. What does fashion reflect in the twenty-first century?

On the minus side, irony. On the plus side, intelligent editing.

- What book would you recommend to every fashion designer?

A good pattern-making manual.

Rick Owens
7 bis, place du Palais-Bourbon
75007 Paris
France
www.rickowens.eu

Rick Owens

Photography by Jera

Photography by Marcelo Krasilic

Spastor

Sergio Pastor and Ismael Alcaina form one of most interesting and promising duos on the Spanish fashion scene. They are one of those creative unions that, without much hullaba-loo, is not only making an international name for itself due to the designers' hard work and quality creations, but is also contributing to the reinvention of a masculine aesthetic identity.

The Spastor man suggests a frontier, extremely alluring masculinity, a somewhat androgy-nous identity with a slightly melancholic, occasionally sinister air that gives rise to the figure of a distinguished yet rather disturbing male: a kind of dandy out of an Edgar Allen Poe tale that situates himself between the darkness and the light in the desperate search for beauty. A radical proposal in which sensitivity does not imply effeminateness or weakness, nor does it require any explication whatsoever regarding sexual orientation.

The Spastor label was born in 1995, and the following year the design duo presented its collection on the Pasarela Gaudí fashion runway in Barcelona. Since then, these two de-signers have been working nonstop. In Spain in 2001, they were awarded the L'Oréal prize for the best collection. Beyond their national borders, they have presented their pret-a-porter collections at the Galerie Gilles Peyroulet & Cie, in 2003, and the Espace Hexamo in París, in 2004, as well as at Paris Men's Fashion Week in January 2005. Currently, the focus of their work lies beyond native frontiers in the search for wider vistas that will allow them to continue growing in the manner they wish. The success they have had with singers such as Marilyn Manson, who wore one of their suits to his wedding with Dita Von Teese, Patrick Wolf and Rammstein attest to the fact that they are on the right track.

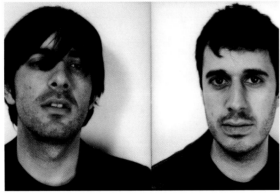

Photography by Daniel Riera

Photography by Biel Sol

Collection "From Behind" (Spring/ Summer 2007), presented at Paris Menswear Fashion Week and Cibeles Madrid Fashion Week, in which the color black, the highest quality material, details in red, balls, crystal buttons, and silk linings abound.

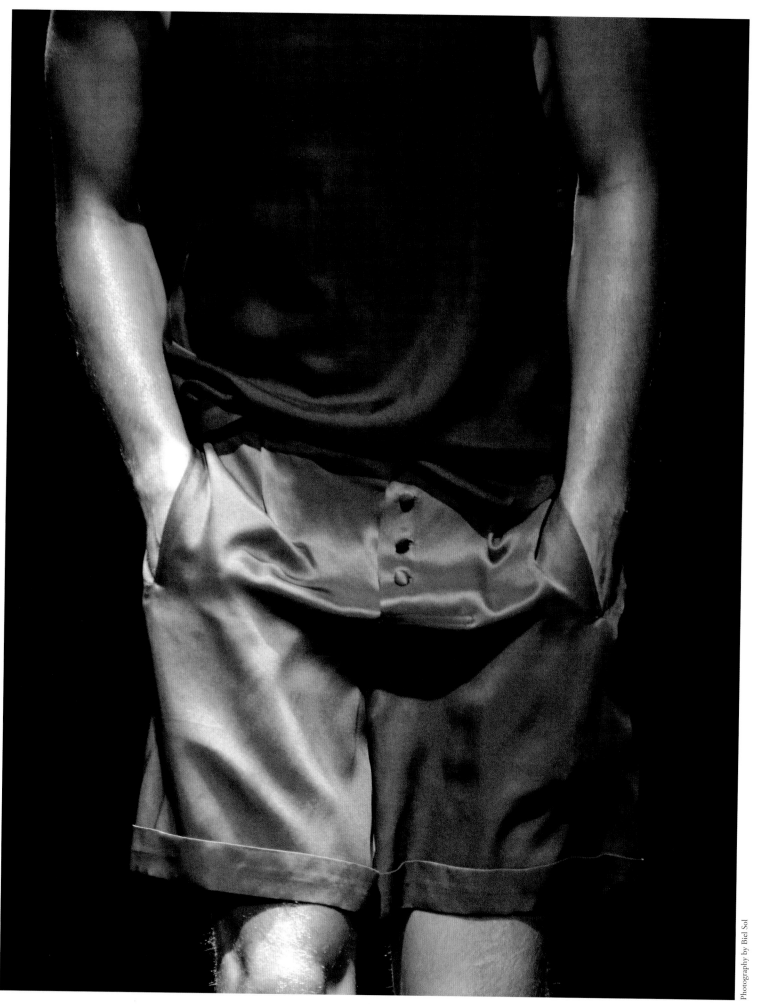

Photography by Biel Sol

- What inspires you?

As Felipe Salgado said, our collections are a fragmentary yet consistent reflection of our personality—of our tastes, myths, phobias—presented as an indeterminate and relative truth.

- What is your dream as designers?

To continue enjoying our work.

- What has been the most important achievement in your career?

Learning what we want and, more importantly, what we don't want.

- How important are trends?

For what we do, they're insignificant.

- Fashion has always reflected a certain era. What does fashion reflect in the twenty-first century?

The time of revisions, mythifications and globalized individualizations.

- What book would you recommend to every fashion designer?

One that we keep on our nightstand: *The Foolish Children*, by Ana María Matute.

Spastor
Méndez Núñez, 1, 2º, 2ª
08003 Barcelona
Spain
www.spastor.org

Photography courtesy of Spastor

Photography by Wade H. Grimbly

In blue, white and black tones that move
gradually from the softness of sky blue
to the rotundity of jet-black, Spastor
presented his Spring/Summer 2006
collection, titled "Arde," in Barcelona
and Paris, the latter being a city where
his work was very well received.

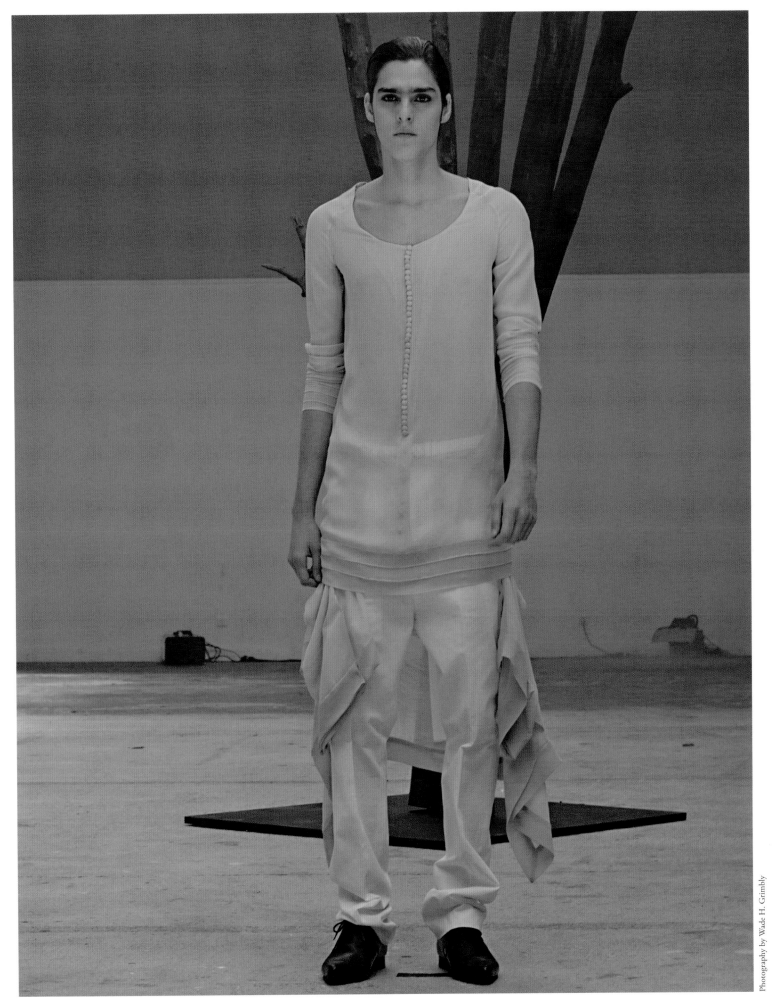

Photography by Wade H. Grimbly

Photography courtesy of Sun Goddess

Sun Goddess

Sun Goddess is more than a brand; it is a declaration of purpose—the firm intention to situate South Africa in the world of fashion at long last in a durable and honest way without sacrificing roots or foregoing trends radiating from the neurological centers of fashion.

This label is the fruit of the knowledge of what identity and fashion mean in an image-saturated society, of the understanding that fashion is an excellent vehicle for the creation of identities, of the awareness that recognition of the elegance of African aesthetics is fundamental to a strategy aimed at creating value in a world that craves authenticity, of the sense that fashion connects with something larger, with personal style, and that fashion is in fact the radiography of cultural identity, of a position in the world.

For all of the above, Mr. and Mrs. Mangaliso founded Sun Goddess less than ten years ago with the clear purpose of participating in the reconstruction of their country's identity while simultaneously referencing what they consider to be its glorious past, one which they hope to recover with pride and joy through their creations.

Sun Goddess came into being with the hope of providing and exporting the experience of luxury and African style through clothes, accessories and perfumes. The brand, in addition, has a new, indispensable business line for marketing fashion, one of an advisory nature regarding African imagery for different sales lines. All of this makes Sun Goddess a kind of visual consultant whose aim is to communicate Africa to the world. Clothing conceived for African goddesses but accessible to women of this world.

Photography courtesy of Sun Goddess

Photography courtesy of Sun Goddess

Few labels have as clear a brand philosophy
as Sun Goddess, created to demonstrate to
the world of African creativity, the beauty
of African culture, the continent's ancestral
richness, and, more than anything, the
pride of being African. Images from the
Spring/Summer 2008 collection.

Photography courtesy of Sun Goddess

- What inspires you, Mr. Mangaliso?

A lot of things: working with people, cutting clothes, designing clothes, combining materials, different kind of materials.

- What is your dream as a designer?

Having my own company and working with great people.

- What has been the most important achievement of your career?

Designing for my own label.

- How important are trends?

If I can take trends, I make it. I prefer to create for everyone.

- Fashion has always reflected a certain era. What does fashion reflect in the twenty-first century?

In my case, it reflects African culture, the African feeling, and it wants to be fashion for everybody, black or white.

- What book would you recommend to every fashion designer?

Pattern books. You can find fashion in every book; every book includes fashion.

Sun Goddess
Regent @ The Zone, 2nd floor
177 Oxford Street, Rosebank 2196
South Africa
www.sungoddess.co.za

Sun Goddess

Photography courtesy of Sun Goddess

Photography courtesy of Sun Goddess

Photography courtesy of Sun Goddess

Images from the Spring/Summer 2008
collection. The South African label
carries out continuous research in
close collaboration with the Tshwane
University of Technology, with the
objective of making unique fabrics that
reflect the value of African culture.

Susan Cianciolo

Still photo of the film *1960s Butterfly Girl* taken by Todd Cole in Malibu

Susan Cianciolo

The work of Susan Cianciolo is porous, one that goes beyond frontiers, given the influence of art and the bombardment of stimuli to which New Yorkers are constantly subjected. For this reason, it is difficult to define her style without betraying the spirit of hybridization and resistance to categorization for which the artist is known. Still, if pressed to say something, the fairest thing would be to describe the artist as she describes herself: a designer who also makes art, and a conceptual artist who occasionally designs clothes. This vague yet fruitful attitude has made her work a privileged passage through fashion, art, society and nature, or in other words, through life itself. One might say that her work is dirty work, in the sense that it is soaked through with everything going on around it and utterly removed from the pretense of timeless cosmetic cleanliness that populates showcase windows. The clothes of Susan Cianciolo are for living well, and life runs through this designer's creations.

Susan studied fashion design in New York and Paris. After returning from Europe, she launched X-Girl in collaboration with Sonic Youth bassist (and painter) Kim Gordon. After that, her work emerged as an ongoing dialog with her surroundings. The result of such contextual involvement are garments that, created from recycled material, back up this commitment to one's immediate environment and demonstrate that beauty resides not only in exclusive luxury but can be created out of what is left over, from what others reject, through change and transformation. These are garments which demonstrate that, in the face of an industry that produces accessories and new sales at a voracious pace, there exists an intelligent, aesthetic and stimulating form of creation. Welcome to the culture of hybridization, welcome to the twenty-first century.

Photography by Vanina Sorenti

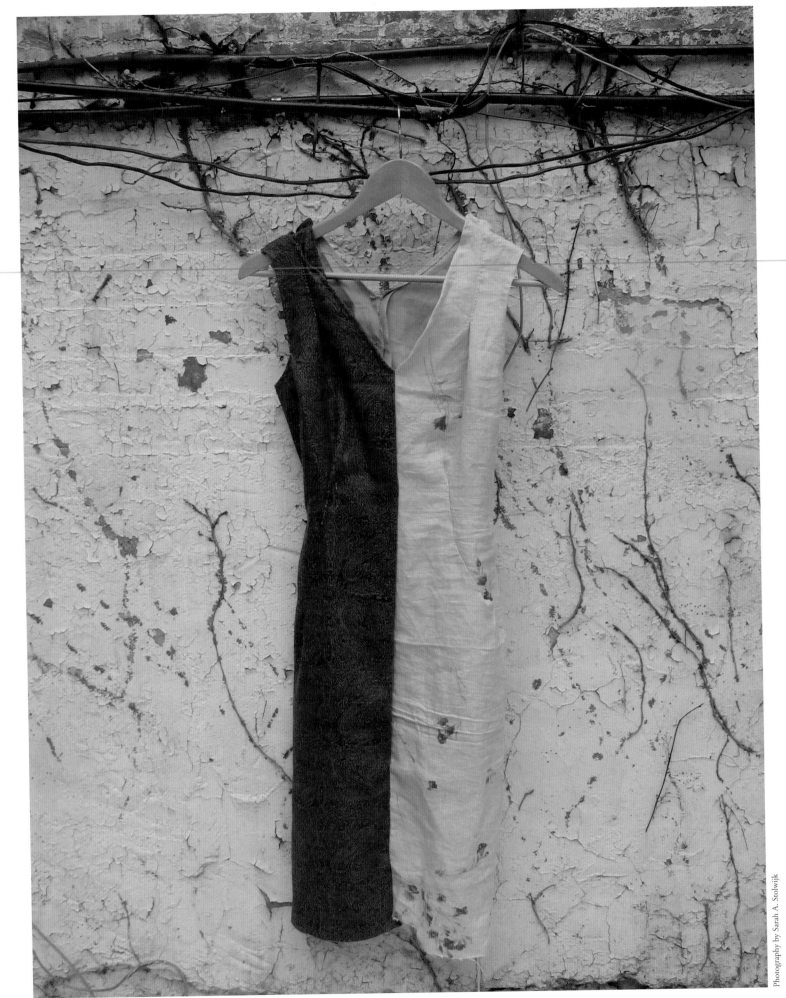

Photography by Sarah A. Stolwijk

Two dresses from the "Queen of Hearts" collection, which is based on seventeenth-century stories of princesses who outfitted the interior of their dresses with small pockets to hold essences.

Photography by Sarah A. Stolwijk

- What inspires you?

Certain films, museums like MASS MoCA, abstract installations, Sister Corita, Native Americans, music like The Sads, plant life, animals and forests.

- What is your dream as a designer?

To design for a couture fashion house and also to create costumes for a ballet and opera; to do a show at the Guggenheim.

- What has been the most important achievement of your career?

Three retrospectives: Eindhoven (Holland), Tokyo, and Milan, and the exhibition entitled Run Restaurant.

- How important are trends?

It is two-sided; they are very important to shape an era, and they are not important when it is something we follow!

- Fashion has always reflected a certain era. What does fashion reflect in the twenty-first century?

This is the century of everything; anyone as a creator can do any form of design. Fashion is open to everyone, like athletes and actors. We have a high level of stimulation; fashion comes in all forms and comes at you from all angles. It is a higher level of making a statement.

- What book would you recommend to every fashion designer?

There is not one for me to say; each designer is so unique.

Susan Cianciolo
175 East Broadway #3A
New York, NY 10002
United States
www.susancianciolo.com

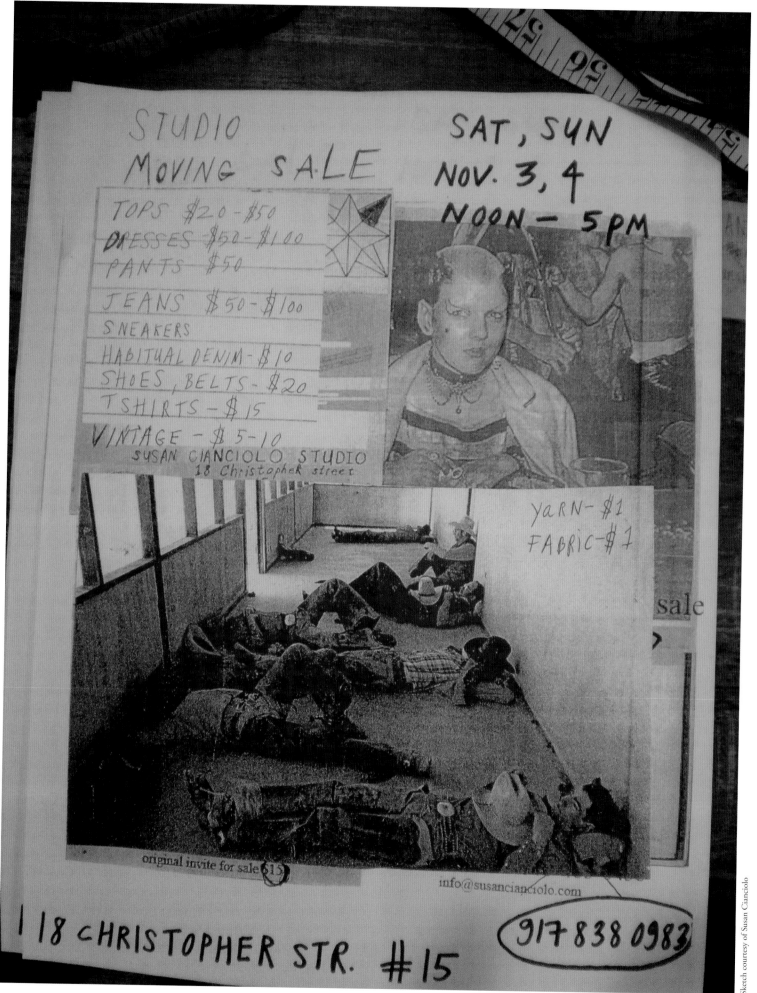

STUDIO
MOVING SALE

SAT, SUN
NOV. 3, 4
NOON - 5PM

TOPS $20 - $50
DRESSES $50 - $100
PANTS $50
JEANS $50 - $100
SNEAKERS
HABITUAL DENIM - $10
SHOES, BELTS - $20
TSHIRTS - $15
VINTAGE - $5 - 10
SUSAN CIANCIOLO STUDIO
18 Christopher street

YARN - $1
FABRIC - $1

sale

original invite for sale $15

info@susanciancolo.com

118 CHRISTOPHER STR. #15

917 838 0983

Sketch courtesy of Susan Cianciolo

demo #3

Books
high stack

TABLE 2 II

TAB

anciolo: Andrea Rosen Gallery, NYC; Gallery 360°, Tokyo.

Sketch courtesy of Susan Cianciolo

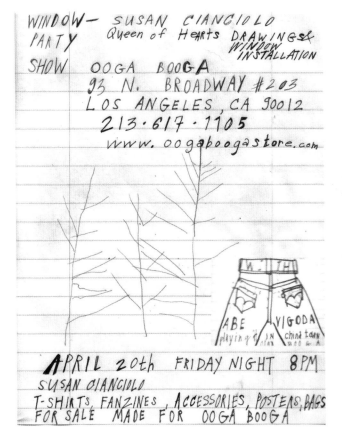

Sketch courtesy of Susan Cianciolo

Two illustrations by Susan Cianciolo.
Above, the invitation for one of her
presentation parties, done on a simple
sheet of notebook paper.

Photography by Gatti

Sybilla

The creations of Sybilla evoke a unique yet oddly universal world, an iconic and elemental one that possesses an air of timelessness. For this reason, the inclusion of Sybilla in this volume was a must, as her designs combine the best tailoring with originality and simplicity, successfully evincing the richness of the austere through dresses, suits, sandals and shirts free of pomp and artifice.

There is something imprecise in Sybilla's garments, something that transmits an essence remote from the ephemeral, fluctuating trends that usually prevail in fashion. One might argue that they embody an austere, Castilian elegance. Her sober, rounded dresses gathered up by pleats possess a certain mystical air. In short, there is a sophisticated simplicity free of ostentation that, tinged with a palette of vibrant colors, acquires a pictorial exquisiteness. It is no surprise, then, that in the fall of pure red and white dresses and the vivacity of black and green capes, we recognize the tonal brilliance of El Greco and the colors of Flemish painting.

This is what makes Sybilla's clothes so special, lasting and such a smashing commercial success in the fashion industry. Evolving naturally without brusque turns or drastic changes in direction, she has imbued everything from homeware to jewelry and accessories with an animistic spirit.

Photography by Anton Goudi

Photography by Gatti

From left to right: images from the
2000, 2001 and 2002 collections.
These garments inspire faith in the
imperishable nature of the work of a
designer who has achieved something
only great ballerinas know how to do:
dance in such a way that it looks easy.

Photographies by Gatti

- What inspires you?

Inspiration comes from everyday life, being in love, nature, silence. I find what I'm looking for playing around with fabrics or materials. Even if I usually don't know what it is, I recognize it when I'm there.

- What is your dream as a designer?

Clean production systems that are sustainable and fair, to indulge in beauty without limits, to make nomadic houses made of fabrics, and so much more…

- What has been the most important achievement of your career?

All the tours I took, the times I stopped, changed, disappeared, blew everything up to come back with passion again in a new way.

- How important are trends?

I tend to do what feels right. I'm not much aware of what's going on in the fashion world.

- Fashion has always reflected a certain era. What does fashion reflect in the twenty-first century?

Unfortunately, looking at the mainstream, lack of individualism, the triumph of multinationals, the manipulation of people. But there is the freedom of expression, the end of rules, innovation, comfort.

- What book would you recommend to every fashion designer?

La vie des abeille's and *La vie des fourmis*, by Maurice Maeterlinck, and *Like Water for Chocolate*, by Laura Esquivel. They don't talk about fashion; they talk about "gut-creation" instinct, sensuality, the force of nature. For me, that is what is at the core of fashion.

Sybilla
Callejón de Jorge Juan, 12
28001 Madrid
Spain
www.sybilla.es

Photography by Gatti

Photography by Gatti

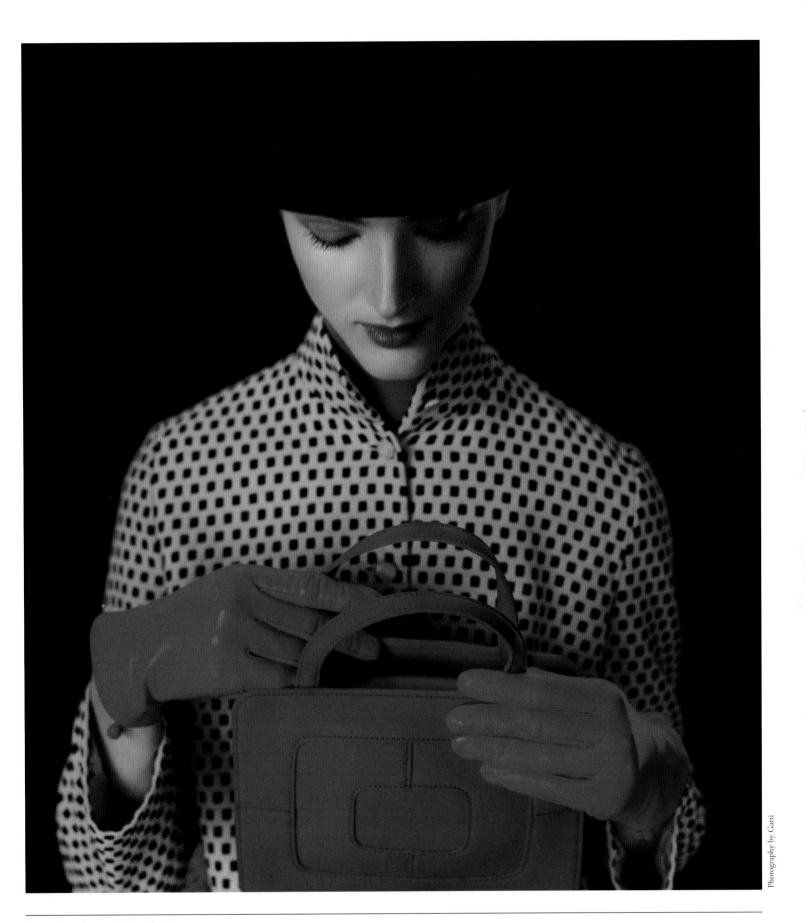

Photography by Gatti

Images from the years 1997 and 1999.
As Sybilla herself has acknowledged,
her work is an attempt to reconcile
theoretically divergent elements: sensibility and extravagance, humor and
elegance, surprise and discretion.

Photography by Chloe Mallet

Temperley London

In record time, Temperley London has become one of the most internationally successful labels in British fashion. Proof is not only that stars of the caliber of Scarlett Johansson and Natalie Portman are crazy about Temperley London dresses, but the electrifying growth of the brand, reflected in the scope of its expansion: 290 boutiques in thirty-five countries in less than seven years. From Harrods and Harvey Nichols in the United Kingdom to Neiman Marcus and Saks Fifth Avenue in New York, not to mention 10 Corso Como, everyone is interested in having Temperley London in their store.

This label's commercial success is the result of the quality and excellent skills of its designer. Alice Temperley studied at Central Saint Martins in London. There she specialized in textile technology and printing processes, convinced that mastery of these areas would open up new avenues in creation and design. And such was the case, as her expertise in these departments brought her early recognition and a slew of awards, including the Innovation Prize given by Central Saint Martins.

It is no accident, then, that one finds in her garments a taste for work well done, for meticulous dressmaking that brings together the most traditional processes and the most complex and innovative techniques.

This blend of quality, aesthetics and technical rigor has resulted in an extraordinary label, one that is astounding both in the commercial and visual sense. She is nothing less than an international reference of British fashion.

Photography courtesy of Temperly London

Photography by Alexi Lumomirski

Fall/Winter 2007–2008 collection inspired by the Russian emigration to Paris following the Revolution, as the above design attests to in the form of a short skirt and jacket. To the right, a different line: an orange dress with Byzantine-style gold ornaments.

Photography by Alexi Lumomirski

- What inspires you?

Everything around me: travel, music, film and my large library of things I have collected since I was a child.

- What is your dream as a designer?

To be able to have the time to continue to do what I enjoy. I think it is very important to keep your vision and identity as you grow. Also, I would love for these clothes to be treasured and worn for years to come, to survive the tests of time, timeless and well-made.

- What has been the most important achievement of your career?

To still be here, doing what I enjoy.

- How important are trends?

I do not follow trends. If you are following trends, then they must be already around and therefore already dated. Designers work so far in advance that they should follow their vision, not a trend prediction. Too many people are obsessed with following or hitting trends. Fashion design should be about individuality.

- Fashion has always reflected a certain era. What does fashion reflect in the twenty-first century?

Unfortunately, it has become faster and faster and louder and louder. In my view, less time is being spent on the craft and on making beautiful things. It is all about who has the biggest marketing budget, who puts on the craziest show. To me, all of this is less about beauty; it is less about the wearer. It is about egos and big business, and that is a worrying trend. On the other hand, fashion has gotten a much broader audience, meaning that people in general care more about an important part of life. Clothes and other fashion accessories have an influence on how you feel and how you are perceived. More accessibility in that respect is a good thing. Also, it seems that at least the developed markets are less ruled by labels and big brands. People are getting more individual; they better understand what design and quality is about and are less directed by marketing ploys and insecurity. That is a good trend, and I hope it continues. Of course, there is also a strong experimental side to fashion in the twenty-first century, and that is needed to advance things. However, I feel there is a general focus back onto what really matters to people when they choose their fashion. In my view, while interesting to watch, the space age/experimental lady that is currently being portrayed is going to be a very lonely lady. I hope that fun, wildness and beauty win in the twenty-first century—a renaissance of style and beauty.

- What book would you recommend to every fashion designer?

Fashion in Film, by Engelmeier.

Temperley London
6-10 Colville Mews, Lonsdale Road
London W11 2DA
United Kingdom
www.temperleylondon.com

Photography courtesy of Temperly London

Photographies courtesy of Temperly London

In these images, we can observe the
creative process Temperley garments go
through in the studio. While not quite
a baroque designer, Alice Temperley
has a pronounced affection for lavish
detail.

Photography courtesy of Temperly London

Photography by James Ryang

Thom Browne

Thom Browne's clothing is fashioned with care and delicacy, everything orchestrated with a meticulousness that exhibits exquisite tastes free of pretense. His designs are directed at a male audience desirous of a spectacular look beyond clichés and commonalities, an elegant, impeccable, deliciously transgressive appearance.

His suits are the evident result of his influences, from the tailoring techniques of the 30s and 40s to the stamp left by his having worked for Ralph Lauren: the mythic designer's signature notion of American culture and its perpetual reinvention.

All of this made Thom the deserving recipient of the 2006 Council of Fashion Designers of America prize for the best men's clothing, a prestigious acknowledgement of a career that began in New York, where this magnificent designer came to work in the Giorgio Armani showroom. This was followed by his work for Ralph Lauren on the Club Monaco line, which lasted for several years before he founded his own company.

His debut was in 2001, and since then, the designs of Thom Browne have come to encompass the entire male wardrobe: T-shirts, underwear, ties. A few years later, he crossed the masculine frontier and began designing clothes for women, as well. This was thanks to Brooks Brothers, the famous and traditional North American brand that proposed that Browne come up with a capsule collection for women as part of its recently inaugurated creative concept laboratory. More than anything, the work of Thom Browne is a personal homage to lovers of individual, elegant style, a luxury for the culture of the ephemeral.

Photography by Marcelo Krasilic

Photography by Dan & Corina Lecca

Browne presented this Fall/Winter 2006 collection on a skating rink in order to express his vision of the traditional male wardrobe: garments conceived for movement and a public that accepts his idea of tailoring as a form of avant-gardism and rebellion.

545
Thom Browne

Photography by Dan & Corina Lecca

- What inspires you?

Real people.

- What is your dream as a designer?

To provoke different ideas.

- What has been the most important achievement of your career?

Each and every collection is an important achievement for me.

- How important are trends?

For me, trends are not important at all.

- Fashion has always reflected a certain era. What does fashion reflect in the twenty-first century?

I don't really follow what other designer are doing, but for me it reflects keeping true to one's ideas. Having individuality is very important.

- What book would you recommend to every fashion designer?

The Fountainhead.

Thom Browne
100 Hudson Street
New York, NY 10013
United States
www.thombrowne.com

Photographies by James Ryang

Photography by Dan & Corina Lecca

Photography by Dan & Corina Lecca

Bermudas, suit jackets and empire-style
tuxedoes, along with unusual lengths
in sleeves and pants, are some of the
basic concepts of the Fall/Winter 2007
collection of this new New York dandy
of the twenty-first century.

Timothy Everest

Photography by Kevin Davies

Timothy Everest

Timothy Everest is one of the best representatives of the renovation in tailoring that seeks to grant a contemporary and progressive touch to a trade which, for years, has been bound to tradition and craftsmanship.

Timothy's impeccable and punctilious work is directed at customers seeking both elegance and sophistication. He is sensitive enough to appreciate the sober grace of good tailoring while seasoning it with a touch of color or an unusual accessory. For this reason, musicians, artists, actors and many other clients have visited his Georgian workshop in Spitalfields in search of an exquisite suit with a personality all its own. This ingenious tailor received his first commission in 1989, followed by his first pret-a-porter collection in 1999. Since then, he has been met with unceasing success, combining work on his own projects with that for other brands and labels like Marks & Spencer, whose "Autograph" line he has collaborated on for some time, or designer Kim Jones, whose successful Spring/Summer 2005 collection he also contributed to, or the denim suits he created for Levi's.

Everything that Timothy puts his hands on becomes a standard for quality, innovation and good taste. A balance between the classical and the contemporary, between research and the legacy of tailoring. An ingenious artisan not afraid to explore beyond the limits of the known, a trait exemplified by his foray into the increasingly expansive Asian market. A designer without frontiers whose far-reaching vision allows him to explore new avenues for reinterpreting a trade so traditional it must situated ahead of its time.

Photography courtesy of Timothy Everest

Sketch courtesy of Timothy Everest

In the first sketch, a knee-length button-down town coat with concealed fly front opening and bespoke detail cuff. In the second, a single-breasted two-button jacket with double-jetted half-moon pockets and a four-button cuff.

Sketch courtesy of Timothy Everest

Timothy Everest

- Are you responsible for all the creative direction, or is it shared with a creative team?

Yes, it's my creative direction.

- What percentage of you is a designer and what percentage a tailor?

I would say it is 50/50, in the sense that I think it is important that we are tailors who design, not designers who have discovered tailoring.

- Is the main aim of Timothy Everest the worship to detail?

Yes, we worship detail. It is very important. Tailoring is all about attention to detail and what might need adjustment. Those little things that are very subtle are very important.

- Which are the advantages of being tailor when designing a collection?

The advantage is actually knowing about shape proportion, fit and how garments go together. We have people that are very good at drawing and can design ideas but would not necessarily be able to put them together. It is a big advantage to be able to put things together, but also to understand how they are all built in order to make a much better garment, a much better look.

- The selection of fabrics is a crucial part of designing a collection. How do you develop this process?

We constantly evolve the fabrics that we use; our benchmark has always been very British, but it also has an element of luxury, and Susan and I are always looking for new things. For example, we were looking for tweed for the autumn-winter away and we managed to find some tweed in Japan, tweed yarn mixed with denim yarn that ended in something traditional but very modern.

- Which can be the course of tailoring? Can it walk beside fashion or, as it happened in some countries, does it run the risk of disappearing under the dressmaking industry?

When we started the business, tailoring was in great danger of disappearing, but fortunately now it is probably more popular than it has been for a long time. The problem is the craft and the custom made is becoming smaller and smaller. Having said that, "ready to wear" is becoming very popular just in time. You are talking about fashion versus tailoring. It's talking about something very individual; it's for that person. After the influences of the 60s and the 80s in fashion, there is really nothing very new, so I think tailoring it is a great vehicle, because the only way to be modern it is to be yourself, and tailoring is a big expression of that.

Timothy Everest

Unit B24 Corbet Place

London E1 6NH

United Kingdom

design@timothyeverest.co.uk/www.timothyeverest.co.uk

Timothy Everest

Sketch courtesy of Timothy Everest

TIMOTHYEVEREST
details

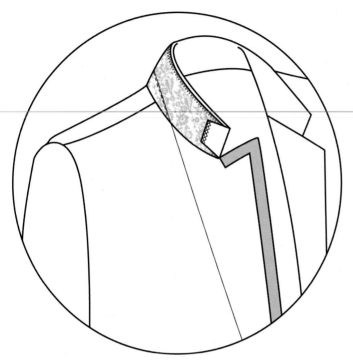

Trim print on under side of lapel

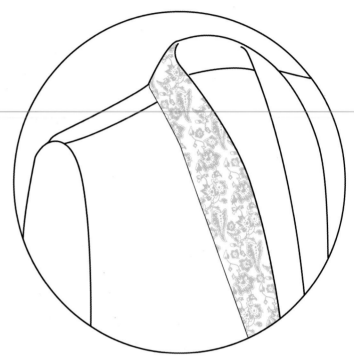

Trim print on under side of shawl collar

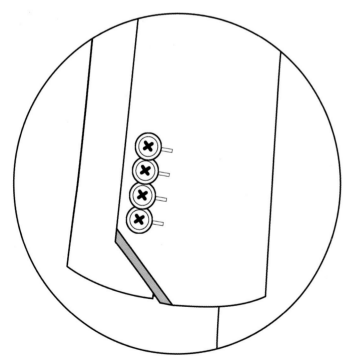

Trim on chiselled cuff

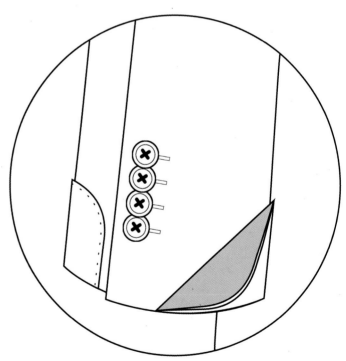

Turnback cuff with trim detail

Sketch courtesy of Timothy Everest

Photographies by David Goldman/styling: James Sleaford/model: Simon Blackford

On the left, detailed illustrations of
lining concealed in the lapels and collar,
as well as different kinds of hems for
jacket sleeves. Above, two designs.

Photography by Chris Moore

Unconditional

The creations of Unconditional communicate a distinguished comfort, an air of serenity, as if the slightest gesture of the person wearing them were enough to radiate elegance. All of the garments—pants, skirts, jackets and dresses—are characterized by balance and a fundamental cleanness free of ostentation. For this reason, Unconditional represents another turn of the screw in elegant modernity as a clear example of the magnetism of the simple, of the strength of cuts performed with care, of attention to detail in collections charged with a contemporary attitude, an elegant, urban casual that emerges as a proportionate shadow accompanying the figure of both a woman and a man, thanks to the use of pure colors.

The beginnings of this label were modest. Starting with a small ten-piece capsule for men in 2003, today close to a hundred stores are avid to have its creations in stock. Philip Stephens, the label's soul and founder, first began to define the nature of the brand by paying special attention to the quality of the materials used in his first men's collection. Shortly thereafter, he presented a men's and women's collection together, which led to his becoming an indispensable figure in London fashion.

Designs with pure cuts, clean and forceful colors, the absence of prints and stridency, all oriented toward highlighting the personality of the person wearing them, yet they do so stealthily, without exaggerated displays of emotion. Perhaps this is the reason why it is the label chosen by David Bowie, Michael Stipe, Kate Moss, Tori Amos and Gwen Stefani. Perhaps for this same reason it is one of the brands having the most impact on British fashion today.

Photography courtesy of Unconditional

The above image belongs to the Spring/
Summer 2007 collection; the one on
the right is from the Fall/Winter 2006–
2007 collection. Both designs share
three of the fundamental features of
the garments of Unconditional: clean,
sensual and super-easy-to-wear.

Photography by Chris Moore

Photography by Chris Moore

- What inspires you?

Nature constantly inspires me as a designer—it will never be surpassed. The energy of London inspires me in lots of ways. The process of travel is often very inspirational for some reason, maybe because one is taking in so much new information. Sometimes I find new technology really exciting; other times I find it really depressing.

- What is your dream as a designer?

Hmm... I'd actually really like to redesign Virgin Airlines uniforms! They really don't express in any way the Virgin vision or experience, of which I am a great fan!

- What has been the most important achievement of your career?

Selling and then delivering the very first order on time!

- How important are trends?

I would like to say that they are not, but of course trends are subliminally affecting us all to one extent or another in everything we experience, from graphics to interiors to music to packaging. It's impossible not to be influenced by them. What's good is to let them lead you off into new worlds, to open up new possibilities and ideas.

- Fashion has always reflected a certain era. What does fashion reflect in the twenty-first century?

Well, we are only seven years into the twenty-first century, so that's a bit difficult to say yet, no? But one would hope twenty-first-century fashion will see a continued increase in choice of all styles at one time and a continued demand for comfort and a relaxing of dress codes. I think menswear has seen and will continue to see much more change than women's wear. I guess a new layering, techno-natural fabrics, recycling (including "vintage") and the necessary green issues will all be the topics that will shape twenty-first-century fashion by the end of this century.

- What book would you recommend to every fashion designer?

The Bible!

Unconditional
16 Monmouth Street
London WC2H 9DD
United Kingdom
philip@concretelondon.com

Photography by Chris Moore

563
Unconditional

Photography by Chris Moore

Photography by Chris Moore

Spring/Summer 2007 collection in
which Philip Stephens, founder of the
brand Unconditional, placed his faith
in the range of pale gray colors, with an
occasional sprinkling of brighter tones.

Bubble n
rain hat !

Elastic gather
back midi dress
with deep pockets
back-pack parka
layers —

Veiled fox Print
chiffon toppings

Sketches by Philip Stephens for the
Spring/Summer 2008 collection
presented at London Fashion Week.
Above, green mini-dress with pockets
accompanied by a cape-parka. To the
right, a dress with a wide, elaborate
neck in washed silk.

Sketch courtesy of Unconditional

Sculpture Collar dress
with
Ghost hoody
— below knee dress
with quilted
leather waistband.
in washed silk..

: Saffron + white ?

Sketch courtesy of Unconditional

Photography by Luciana Val & Franco Musso

Vero Ivaldi

Vero Ivaldi

Vero was born in Argentina and studied design and fashion in the Department of Architecture, Design and Urbanism at the Universidad de Buenos Aires. Her christening in the world of fashion came in 1999, in the form of Argentina Fashion Week. Since then, the awards have not stopped: the Argentine Chamber of Fashion prize in the category of Designer Sensation and the Original Design award, the Konex Foundation's prize for one of a hundred outstanding artists, etc. As a result of these awards, she began exporting to the United States, and currently her creations can also be found in the United Kingdom and Chile.

Her training leaves a signature stamp on each one of her designs. The study of the body, its axes and kinetics, serves in the creation of beautiful, comfortable, functional designs. "Ecstatic," "Kinetics," "Inventive," "Operation," and "Optical" are the names of some of her collections in which her interests as an artist and architect come together in unique, innovative proposals.

The product of all this engineering, however, is neither frigid nor stuffy. To the contrary, her designs are feminine, French-like, innocent, and chic. A studied and becoming elegance that molds to the body in the form of dresses and tailored shirts characterized by clean, natural cuts and full skirts. Her style has its foundation in studied patterns and the continuous rethinking of her work, which, contrary to what one might suppose, results in a natural, unadorned style. This has made her one of the most renowned designers in Latin America.

Photography by Matías Corral

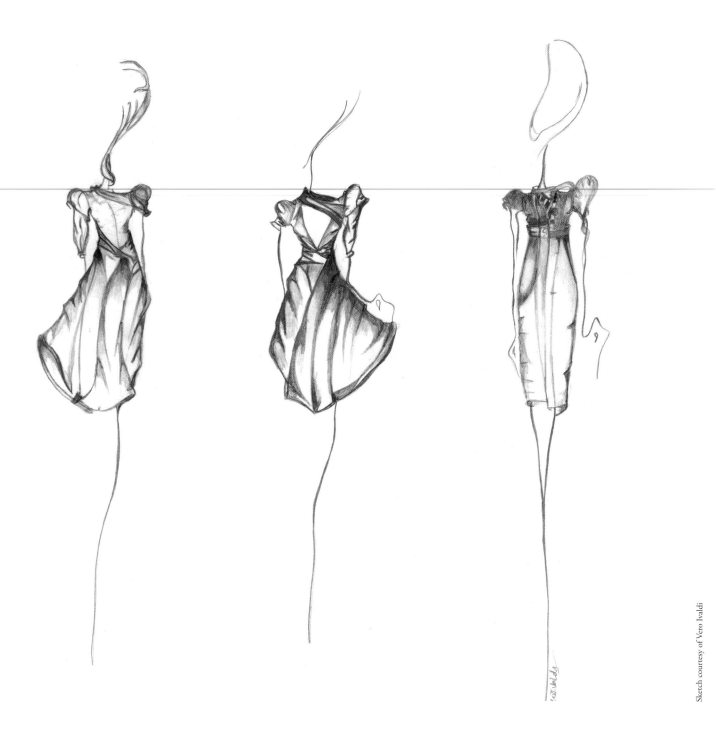

Sketch courtesy of Vero Ivaldi

Photography by: Luciana Val & Franco Musso

To the left, illustration by the Argentinean designer. Above, an image from the Fall/Winter 2006–2007 collection ("Topiario"), staged in a kind of imaginary world somewhere between kitsch and the elegance of the 50s.

- What inspires you?

My work is based on the study of the human body, anthropometry, ergonomics, form, composition and the axes that ultimately give rise to patterns. It's a study of the human body by way of architectural plans, sewing darts that fork off in different directions and result in new paths and fragments.

The theme of each collection has something to do with each moment, with my experiences, longings and needs. After selecting a theme, I begin with a hypothesis that leads to investigation and experimentation, like with my first collection, "Kinetics" (Winter 2001), which, starting with patterns, sought sensation of movement and lightness in rigid textures; or guessing games, which I'm a huge fan of, like *Tetris* ("Ingenuity," Winter 2002) and chess ("Static," Winter 2004); or topiary ("Topiario," Winter 2006), which deals with poetics and the composition of forms; or "Wind" (Winter 2007), which is based on experimentation concerning the impact of wind on garments; or, as in my latest collection (Summer 2008), "Encounter with Magritte." It doesn't only refer to clothes, but has to do with a medium for narrating moments and sensations, for articulating what I am thinking. In each collection, I try to introduce the "other" into my world, into its particular reality. It's the totality of it all—the composition, the actors, the atmosphere, the walk, the music. Each element of the scene forms part of the story; nothing is isolated, nothing is left to chance.

- What is your dream as a designer?

Rather than a dream, I would call them objectives that are met as others emerge.

- What has been the most important achievement in your career?

Taking the chance to always do what I want in my life.

- How important are trends?

Having a hallmark design style requires a personal search, years of work, scientific research, and one's own process. A designer must create his own trend.

- Fashion has always reflected a certain era. What does fashion reflect in the twenty-first century?

Timelessness.

- What book would you recommend to every fashion designer?

I'm very fond of books of patterns from different decades. They're very useful for understanding the figure, form and conception of the body in distinct historical periods.

Vero Ivaldi
Gurruchaga 1585
Buenos Aires, Capital Federal
Argentina
www.veroivaldi.com

Photography by Luciana Val & Franco Musso

Photography by Luciana Val & Franco Musso

Photography by Luciana Val & Franco Musso

In the collection "Animated Present," from the Spring/Summer 2007 season, Vero Ivaldi gives life to a doll somewhere between surrealism and an enchanting Betty Boop sheathed in a black bubble mini-dress.

Images from the collection "Animated Present" (Spring/Summer 2007). Behind an apparent spontaneity lie garments conceived of mathematically to achieve adequate volumes and symmetries.

Photography by Luciana Val & Franco Musso

Photography by Luciana Val & Franco Musso

Vero Ivaldi

Photography by Peter Stigter

Viktor & Rolf

Viktor & Rolf make an unusual yet nonetheless acclaimed pair in the world of fashion. Their creations, like themselves, occupy an exceptional place in an industry where originality is all too often sacrificed in exchange for recognition. Viktor & Rolf have carved out a much-deserved niche for themselves within Parisian haute couture, which they joined step by step in 1998, without betraying their essence, their unbounded sense of humor and their delicate, glamorous elegance.

This unlikely duo met while studying in Arnhem, both graduating in 1992. One year later, as a prelude to their successful career, they received three prizes at the Hyères Festival. After different collaborations and projects, they decided to follow their own path. With the objective of calling attention to the apathy that prevails in the world of fashion, they presented the collection "Viktor & Rolf on Strike," in which they make clear their attitude toward a creative environment that is apathetic, insensitive and utterly lacking in new ideas.

If anything sums up the creations of Viktor & Rolf, it is a rebellious elegance and a penchant for conceptual and unruly volumes combined with an exquisiteness and surreal humor that pervade all of their work. And it is for this reason that Viktor & Rolf are not just special but necessary, for they represent a concave mirror in fashion that gives rise to a personal cosmos, the unreal world of Alice viewed through the looking-glass, which defies all conventional limitations through chic, meticulous elegance.

Photography by Viktor & Rolf

In silver, above, a dress from the Fall/Winter
2006–2007 collection, which was based on
the most conservative clichés of Parisian
fashion. To the right, the design that opened
the Fall/Winter 2008–2009 collection,
a "no" in the form of a pop-up to the
ephemeral nature of current fashion.

Photography by Peter Stigter

Photography by Peter Stigter

- What inspires you?

Our work is autobiographical in the sense that it is based on personal experiences. Fashion itself and our position within the fashion world are also a source of inspiration.

- What is your dream as a designer?

It has always been our dream to become fashion designers, so we are actually living the dream at this moment. Growing up in suburbia in a country where fashion doesn't really exist, the images of fashion in magazines provided an escape from reality. Fashion still has that effect on us. It is a place to dream. We operate in fashion but still feel like monitors, commenting on fashion whilst being part of it at the same time. Fashion is more than just clothes; it is an aura, with a soul of its own.

- What has been the most important achievement of your career?

To be in fashion and stay in fashion. Our last collection, entitled "No," was based on the current fashion climate, where the demands on designers are so high that we question whether it is sustainable at all. We use our creativity to channel our emotions into our work: our collections and the show. These emotions have a wide range, and we firmly believe that through creativity we can transform anything into something beautiful.

- How important are trends?

Trends for us are not important as an inspiration. We do not set out to design something within a trend or to set a trend. We create something because it is at the forefront of our minds and it needs to be expressed.

- Fashion has always reflected a certain era. What does fashion reflect in the twenty-first century?

It is a little early in the century to be able to say that for fashion in general. We are working on building the House of Viktor & Rolf, a twenty-first-century fashion house, with all the elements such an institution entails, but we want to do it on our terms.

- What book would you recommend to every fashion designer?

Your own diary…

Viktor & Rolf
www.viktor-rolf.com

Photographs by Peter Stigter

583
Viktor & Rolf

Photography by Ronald Stoops

584
Walter Van Beirendonck

Walter Van Beirendonck

Walter is a one-of-a-kind fashion designer. His collections are colorful narratives with a clear and optimistic political message, a joyful and contagious performance of flashing effervescent colors that inundates fashion runways like a flood, a torrent of energy that vindicates safe sex and signals the end of the age of terror and fear, and all with an infectious, irreverent sense of humor that dazzles.

His collections display this almost theatrical taste for representation in their titles: "Stop Terrorizing Our World," "Sexclowns," and "Relics from the Future," to name a few—consistent proclamations for making our world a better, happier place. All of this is embodied in designs where prints, wools, loose-fitting dresses, wide pants and all sorts of accessories prevail, combinations charged with irreverence and a sharp sense of humor that transform apparel into an informal urban wardrobe. However, Walter does not create only clothes; he also illustrates his own comic books, for which he has been awarded numerous prizes.

Born in Belgium, he studied at the Academy of Fine Arts in Antwerp. He belongs to the Six from Antwerp school (Dirk Van Saene, Dries Van Noten, Dirk Bikkembergs, Ann Demeulemeester and Marina Yee) that burst onto the international fashion scene in the late 80s and which has had a tremendous influence on the generation of designers that came after it.

Over the course of his career, the designer has pursued an investigative path, giving continuous shape to his personal universe and thus making him one of the designers most responsible for inducing the fashion world to change tack at unexpected moments.

Photography by Ronald Stoops

Sketch by Walter Van Beirendonck

Spring/Summer 2008 collection,
inspired by the notion of change and
the possibility of projecting oneself as
a digital fantasy. "Sexclown," the title
of the collection, combines this fiction
with other classic fascinations of the
Belgian designer such as fetishism.

Photography by Ronald Stoops

- What inspires you?

I get my inspiration from everything that happening around me. And the world is my main inspiration: contemporary cultural and social events happening in our society; art and the energy of contemporary artists; nature, animals and plants; ethnic tribes and rituals; fetishism; color in all its forms and versions is as important an issue as inspiration; art and fashion history; my love… I try to get as much input and as many impressions into my head as possible. That results in the ideas, sketches and fantasies which I then translate into my recognizable signature.

- What is your dream as a designer?

My dream was and is to create and realize my wildest fantasies in my collections, to use fashion as a communication tool, to tell stories and make statements through my collections. It all came through, and I am still very excited to start up the new collection, to be an outsider in the fashion world with an inside respect!

- What has been the most important achievement of your career?

To realize this dream. To change boundaries in men's fashion.

- How important are trends?

For my collections and clients, they are not important at all. Nevertheless, I think they are fascinating. And it makes me happy that, through certain trends, my work is picked up by youngsters, and "youngsters" means "a new generation." I'm happy that I'm not getting gray together with my audience and that I receive interest and respect from this new generation.

- Fashion has always reflected a certain era. What does fashion reflect in the twenty-first century?

In all the collections I have done, I have tried to reflect the feeling of the moment the collection was created. I hate looking back and don't understand designers who are "designing" exact looks and items from past decades. Every decade has its own character and "look," and the clothes that people wear do reflect that. Twenty-first century fashion reflects our society and our way of living. That's what fashion does and that's what I like about fashion—it is the mirror of our society.

- What book would you recommend to every fashion designer?

The book I would recommend is nonexistent. I'm buying new books every week. I'm addicted to them, and I love to discover new things. Recommending just one book wouldn't be realistic!

Walter Van Beirendonck
Henri Van Heurckstrasse 5
2000 Antwerp
Belgium
www.waltervanbeirendonck.com

dick_head

mr._realove

love_bull

sex_clown

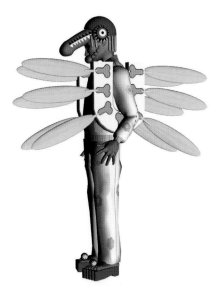

super_cum

body_bear

fuck_face

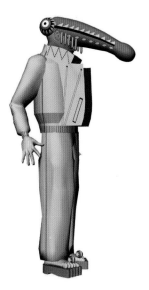

butt_boy

heart_man

sex_angel

W
WORLD

no copy | no trans. | no mod.

Graphic design by Bart Hess

Sketch by Walter Van Beirendonck

Photography by Ronald Stoops

Sketch by Walter Van Beirendonck

Photography by Ronald Stoops

The third fascination that led Walter Van Beirendonck to design "Sexclown" was the *sogobo* tribal rituals of Mali, with marionettes of delirious animal figures like those seen here, as protagonists.

Walter Van Beirendonck

Photography by Ronald Stoops

Photography by Dan & Corina Lecca

592
Yigal Azrouël

Yigal Azrouël

What is it about Israel that allows it to offer up such talented designers as Alber Elbaz and Yigal Azrouël for the world of fashion? Though difficult to pin down precisely, the answer probably has something to do with a special boldness that may correspond to belonging to a culture with an aesthetic vision distinct yet at the same time not excessively remote from that of Europe and the United States. Indeed, Israel is a country that is beginning to blossom in terms of design and thus is one that warrants keeping an eye on.

Born in Israel but of Moroccan origin, Yigal Azrouël is a prime example of the self-taught designer who, through reconstructing articles of clothing, learns all the secrets of dressmaking with his sewing machine. At the age of 22, he decided to move to New York in order to fulfill his dream of triumphing in the world of fashion. Despite his lack of any specific training, he found work immediately as a tailor and designer of wedding gowns in a studio, work that quickly allowed his talent to materialize. Some years later, thanks to his sharp sense of detail and his exquisite skill with drapery and cuts, he opened his first showroom and studio in New York's garment district, where he still produces sixty percent of his clothes. His success in this endeavor led him, three years later, to open his first store, also located in the Big Apple.

His restless nature has served as a catalyst for expanding his horizons. In fall 2007, he presented a capsule collection of accessories and made his debut as a designer of men's fashion with the aim of redefining clothing and the concept of sportswear for the modern man.

Photography by Erez Sabag

Photography by Dan & Corina Lecca

Classic, fresh, sexy yet sophisticated designs were the principal players in the Israeli designer's Spring/Summer 2008 collection, which left no doubt that he continues to be a master of the cut and a custodian of detail.

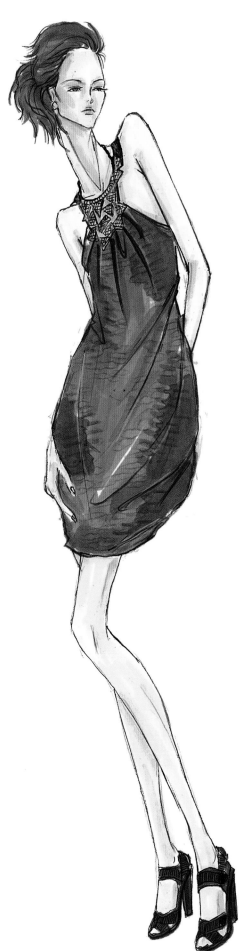

Sketches courtesy of Yigal Azrouël

- What inspires you?

I'm inspired by everything that surrounds me and all of my experiences: travel, architecture, people. For the recent Spring 2008 season, I was drawn to the saturation of 70s American beach culture and surf photography from that era. I've been surfing since childhood; it's a big part of my life and a natural connection in that way.

- What is your dream as a designer?

My dream is to create an atelier that is somehow separate from the business. Of course, I love New York, but to be able to design somewhere a little more isolated, where you can have total serenity and concentrate on just design itself and not worry about industry—that would be perfection.

- What has been the most important achievement of your career?

Opening my boutique in New York's Meatpacking District and having the ability to present my design in my own context and personal aesthetic was a great high point. It's very important for me to have the collections represented in their own natural setting.

- How important are trends?

I don't follow trends.

- Fashion has always reflected a certain era. What does fashion reflect in the twenty-first century?

A global vision. Fashion is at the most exciting point in history, because it is limitless and infinite. It's very individual and plural.

- What book would you recommend to every fashion designer?

The End of Fashion: How Marketing Changed the Clothing Business Forever, by Teri Agins.

Yigal Azrouël
225 West 39th Street, 7th floor
New York, NY 10018
United States
www.yigal-azrouel.com

Yigal Azrouël

Photography by Dan & Corina Lecca

Sketches courtesy of Yigal Azrouël

Yigal Azrouël has known how to adapt very well to North American tastes: simple, always functional, yet with a touch of sophistication. The adaptability of garments to life is paramount, not the other way around. Image from the Spring/Summer 2008 collection and sketches.

Photography by Dan & Corina Lecca

Dedication

This book is dedicated to my parents, Josechu and Cristina, and my grandparents, Joaquín, Lucía, José and Manuela.

Acknowledgments

To my sister for her unconditional support; to my brother José, my family and my friends; to Jorge Lozano, Enrique Loewe, Brenda Chávez, Cheles Tordesillas, Silvia Izquierdo, Alma Fernández Arias, Natalia Culebras, David Flame, Pier Paolo Giordano, Patricia Yagüe and everyone else who assisted me in the writing of this book.